NATIONAL GEOGRAPHIC DIRECTIONS

A Writer's House in Wales

JAN MORRIS

A Writer's House in Wales

NATIONAL GEOGRAPHIC DIRECTIONS

NATIONAL GEOGRAPHIC
Washington D.C.

Published by the National Geographic Society
1145 17th Street, N.W., Washington, D.C. 20036-4688

Library of Congress Cataloging-in-Publication Data

Morris, Jan, 1926-
    A writer's house in Wales / Jan Morris
        p. cm. – (National Geographic directions)
    ISBN 0-7922-6523-8
        1. Wales—Social life and customs. 2. Morris, Jan, 1926—Homes and haunts—Wales. I.
Title. II. Series.

    DA711.5 .M66 2002
    942.9—dc21
                                        2001044731

One of the world's largest nonprofit scientific and educational organizations, the
National Geographic Society was founded in 1888 "for the increase and diffusion of
geographic knowledge." Fulfilling this mission, the Society educates and inspires
millions every day through its magazine, books, television programs, videos, maps
and atlases, research grants, the National Geographic Bee, teacher workshops, and
innovative classroom materials. The Society is supported through membership dues,
charitable gifts, and income from the sale of its educational products. This support is
vital to National Geographic's mission to increase global understanding and promote
conservation of our planet through exploration, research, and education.

www.nationalgeographic.com

Interior design by Michael Ian Kaye, Ogilvy & Mather, Brand Integration Group

Printed in the U.S.A

This small book is certainly not fictional, but it is not all hard fact, either. It describes a writer's home, and it is tempered by a writer's fond imagination. I dedicate it to the two ever-present guardians of the house: Elizabeth who shares it with me, and Wales which is its patron and its inspiration.

—Trefan Morys, 2001

CONTENTS

A Writer's House in Wales

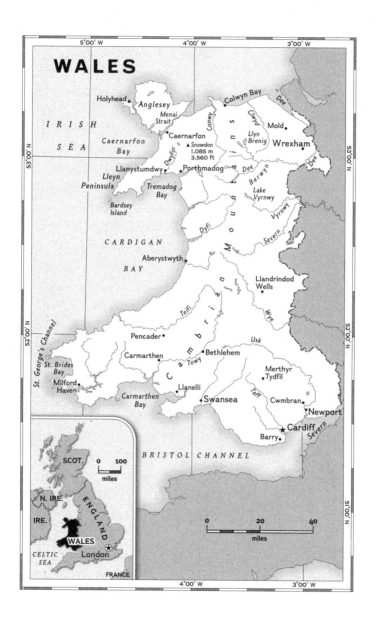

WALES

5°00' W   4°00' W   3°00' W

I R I S H

S E A

Holyhead.

Anglesey

Colwyn Bay

Menai Strait

Mold.

Caernarfon.

▲ *Snowdon* 1,085 m 3,560 ft

Wrexham

Conwy

Clwyd

Llyn Brenig

Caernarfon Bay

53°00' N

Llanystumdwy.

Porthmadog

Dee

Dwyfor

Lleyn Peninsula

Tremadog Bay

Berwyn

Lake Vyrnwy

Bardsey Island

Vyrnwy

Dyfi

M o u n t a i n s

Severn

C A R D I G A N

Aberystwyth.

B A Y

Llandrindod Wells

Wye

52°00' N

Teifi

C a m b r i a n

Pencader.

Usk

Carmarthen.

Bethlehem.

Towy

Merthyr Tydfil.

St. George's Channel

St. Brides Bay

Milford Haven.

Llanelli.

Swansea.

Cwmbran.

Newport.

Taff

Carmarthen Bay

Barry. Cardiff ★

B R I S T O L   C H A N N E L

Severn

SCOT.

0   100
miles

N. IRE.

IRE.

ENGLAND

WALES

London ✪

CELTIC SEA

FRANCE

0   20   40
miles

53°00' N

52°00' N

51°00' N

4°00' W   3°00' W

CHAPTER ONE

A House in Wales

Trefan Morys is the name of my house in Wales, and I'll tell you frankly, to me much the most interesting thing about it is the fact that it *is* in Wales. I am emotionally in thrall to Welshness, and for me Trefan Morys is a summation, a metaphor, a paradigm, a microcosm, an exemplar, a *multum in parvo,* a demonstration, a solidification, an essence, a regular epitome of all that I love about my country. Whatever becomes of Wales, however its character is whittled away down the generations, I hope my small house will always stand in tribute to what has been best in it.

Do you know where Wales is? Most people in the world have no idea. It is a peninsula standing at the heart of the British Isles, on the western flank of England facing Ireland. It is some 200 miles long from north to south and never more than seventy miles wide, and it is known in its own language as Cymru, signifying a comradeship or comity. Wales is part of the United Kingdom, all too often thought by foreigners to be synonymous with England itself, but its people form one of those ancient minority nations, from the powerful Catalans to the infinitesimal Karims, who have miraculously contrived to maintain their identities, to one degree or another, through the infinite convolutions of European history. They are all subject to the political domination of some greater State, but they remain determinedly themselves, and generally hope to stay that way within the framework of a uniting Europe.

Such quixotic survivals suit me. I want no pomp or circumstance, and would much rather be a poet than a President (unless, like Abraham Lincoln, I could be both at the same time). Small may not always be Beautiful, as a mantra of the 1970s used to claim, but for my tastes it is usually more interesting than Large, and little nations are more appealing than great powers. In 1981 the titular Prince of Wales, who has almost nothing to do with the country, and possesses no house in Wales, was married amidst worldwide sycophancy to the future Princess Diana, at Westminster Abbey in London. It was to be a vast display of traditional ostentation, with horses, trumpets, coped ecclesiastics, armed guards, royal standards and all the paraphernalia of consequence, the whole to be transmitted by television throughout the world. I thought it exceedingly vulgar (besides being romantically unconvincing), and with a small band of like-minded patriots decided to celebrate instead an anniversary of our own that fell on the same day. Exactly 900 years before, the Welsh princes Trahaearn ap Caradog and Rhys ap Tewdwr had fought a battle on a mountain called Mynydd Carn, and that's what we chose to commemorate—an obscure substitute perhaps for a televised royal wedding at Westminster, but at least an occasion of our own. We stumbled up that very mountain in a persistent drizzle, and while the entire universe gaped at the splendors in the abbey far away, we huddled there in our raincoats congratulating ourselves upon celebrating a private passion rather than a public exhibition.

Actually national ostentation seems to be gradually going out of fashion even in England. Just as the tanks no longer roll through Red Square on May Day, so formality is fading in royal palaces, even in the most traditionally decorous of them all. I was at a Buckingham Palace reception recently, and when I left I could find no queen, prince or duke to thank for the royal hospitality. I told the policeman at the gate that I had been brought up to say "thank you for having me," but finding nobody inside the house to say it to, would say it to him instead. "Not at all, madam," he at once replied, "come again." Yet if the style of the English monarchy is relaxing, the English nation can never be unpretentious. It is too far gone for that. Simplicity is the prerogative of smaller States, and in particular of the minority nations, like Wales, which are not States at all—by the nature of things, grandeur is seldom their style.

Patriotism, on the other hand, rides high among them. I dislike the word "nationalist," which seems to imply chauvinism or aggressive traits, but I respect honest patriotism everywhere, and I have come to think of myself as a minority patriot, a cultural patriot perhaps—one who believes that the characteristics of a people, however insignificant, a language, a tradition, an ideal, are worth preserving for their own sakes. Political sovereignty may be necessary for the job, but it can be sovereignty essentially defensive, offering no threat to anyone else and chiefly wanting to be left alone. And anyway, since none of these national enclaves has more than a few million people, and none is armed with anything more awful than an air gun, they can hardly go in for bullying.

Wales is not the smallest of Europe's minority nations, with some 2.9 million people, but its history is among the most complex. Almost everything about it, in fact, is convoluted—long-winded, its critics might say—and its self-esteem is considerable. Long before there was such a thing as England the Celtic Welsh people, the Cymry, were the original Britons. They lived all over the island and they followed the druidical animist faith, which was powerful over much of Europe and had some of its supreme sanctuaries in western Britain. The Romans came, eliminating the hostile priesthood of the Druids, and when they withdrew from Britain their cruder Saxon successors drove most of the Cymry out of England into Wales.

There they lived heroically, beating off all assaults, governed by their own princes and noblemen, honoring their own laws, their own values and their own poetical language. Wales was converted to Christianity by wandering missionaries from Ireland, and it developed an indigenous church with a plethora of native saints: St. Teilo and St. Illtyd, St. Pedrog and St. Beuno, Padarn and Cybi and Elian and Curig and Non—Rome never heard of any of them, but they are respected in Wales to this day. For a thousand years the Welsh were alone in the world. England was Saxonized, and lost its Celtic tongue. The Irish were more often enemies than friends. The remaining Celts of northern Britain were cut off and far away. Wales was Wales, ruled by free Welsh princes, cap-a-pie.

In the folk-memory at least it was to be remembered as a golden age, when glittering Welsh aristocrats lived amidst poetry and music, with beautiful women and handsome horses, feasting in high halls and celebrated by bards. Below the ranks of the princes (who very often, I have to admit, quarreled disgracefully among themselves), was a cultivated class of gentry, the *uchelwyr* or noblemen, and the Welsh literature that was born then, mystical, merry, humorous and resplendent, has survived from that day to this. King Arthur himself speaks to us out of that misty Welsh Camelot, and his knights of the Round Table were uchelwyr every one.

It was the Normans, from France, who put an end to the dream. They had taken England for themselves, and soon they were swaggering into Welsh countrysides the Saxons had never entered, and setting up their own rival earldoms all along the English border. They turned thousands of free Welshmen into serfs, they humiliated many a disputatious prince, and in the end, mutating over the generations into Englishmen, they became the masters of Wales. The final Welsh independent ruler,

Llywelyn ap Gruffudd, was killed by the soldiers of Edward I of England in the year 1282, and is remembered by the Welsh still as Llywelyn Ein Llyw Olaf, Llywelyn Our Last Leader. Ever since then Wales has been subject to English domination, sometimes passive beneath the yoke, sometimes restless or obdurate. It has inevitably been Anglicized, like many another English colony, but so far it has remained unmistakably different from its overbearing neighbor, and half a million of its people, the Cymry Cymraeg, still speak Cymraeg, Welsh, by now one of the oldest literary tongues in Europe.

Some Welshmen would claim *the* oldest, but then some Welshmen would claim almost anything for the glory of their country. Pride of race, pride of literature, pride of history, pride of landscape, pride of language, pride of rugby football, pride of singing, pride of kinship and heritage—all these various self-gratifications are endemic among Welsh patriots, and have been irritating or boring their neighbors ever since the English finally conquered the country. For they conquered it, they never extinguished it, and in every generation there have been thousands of Welsh people determined to ensure the survival of Welshness, its language and its culture. They never let up! Skimble-skamble stuff, is how Shakespeare's Henry V characterized Welsh mystical grandiloquence, and to this very day English people are liable to grumble that the Welsh will go on and on...

Go on and on indeed! It is only by going on and on that they have preserved their identity down the ages, confronted so closely by so mighty an alien Power—itself, nowadays, hardly more than an agent for the even more monstrous forces of English-speaking globalization. Much that is most Welsh about Wales goes on and on, or is at least inflated beyond its size. The mountains of Wales, so often celebrated in song and legend, seem much bigger than they really are, if only because they are so often masked in mist and drizzle. The history of Wales, though almost unnoticeable by the standards of the great world, is so snarled about by feud and battle, inheritance and tradition, and so often illuminated by suggestions of the tragic or the arcane, that it can seem a tale of colossi. The melancholy myth of the Welsh coal miners has touched hearts everywhere through film and novel. Welsh poetry is essentially deft, lyrical and limpid—sometimes as minimalist as haiku—but the magical prose tales of Welsh medievalism can be as elaborate in plot and illusion as a biblical epic, and no operatic chorus of slaves, pilgrims or prisoners has ever seemed much more terrific than a

Welsh choir in full-throated, great-hearted, on-and-on-going voice.

Unquenchable down the centuries, then, the spirit of Welsh patriotism has been a devoted and often beautiful abstraction. Long after Llywelyn the Last was dead it burst into a final full-scale rising, led by the charismatic Owain Glyndŵr in the fifteenth century. Glyndŵr united most of Wales behind him in his struggle against the English, summoning a national parliament, striking up an alliance with the French, and fighting on through triumph and chagrin until he faded into oblivion, his grave undiscovered to this day. His hopeless grasp at glory did Wales no practical good, but it has remained always an inspiration in the national memory. So have the words of a venerable citizen known to tradition as The Old Man of Pencader. One day in the twelfth century, it seems, this ancient was standing at the gate of his house when King Henry II of England rode by with a troop of soldiers, in the course of one punitive campaign or other. The king condescendingly inquired, as kings do, whether the old man thought Welsh resistance to England was likely to last, but he got a dusty answer. Wales would never be subdued by the wrath of man, the Old Man said, unless the wrath of God concurred, and "no other nation than this of Wales, in any other language, whatever may hereafter come to pass, shall on the day of supreme examination before the Supreme Judge, answer for this corner of the earth."

I hope he was right, but of course like everywhere else modern Wales is threatened more than ever by the levelling powers of internationalism, distributed even here through every possible channel of communication. The world's corrosion is inevitably setting in—beside the welcome new comforts and excitements, the dross of television and advertising, drugs, crime, general dumbing-down and sheer *ordinariness*. Even the Welshest parts of Wales are less Welsh than they used to be, and the values that Welsh people consider peculiarly their own are being whittled away, or so influenced by ideas and principles from elsewhere that cynics wonder if there really are any specific Welsh values at all. The English language is ubiquitous here nowadays, and so are English people, seeping in as settlers and entrepreneurs into almost every corner of the country their forebears failed to expunge. There have been times when it has seemed, to the Welshest of the Welsh, that everything of theirs was being overwhelmed and obliterated by the English—the bloody Saxon, the Saeson, the eternal enemy.

It is a little like Tibet. Geographically, even historically, Tibet is undeniably part of the Chinese landmass, but its cultural identity is just as undeniably separate, and its people feel their religion, their language, their whole way of life to be threatened by the influx of Han Chinese from the east. Also analogous is what used to be called Palestine. Wales is about the same size as the Holy Land, and in many ways its modern history has not been unlike an ironic cross between the history of the Palestinian Arabs and the history of the Palestinian Jews. On the one hand the Welsh have had to resist, as the Arabs have, the incursion of a more advanced and confident people—foreigners to themselves, as the Jews were foreigners to the Arabs. On the other hand they have been fighting to sustain, like the Palestinian Jews, a proud and ancient culture against an unsympathetic majority.

Outsiders have often considered these attitudes mere sophistry. Are not Arabs and Jews equally Semitic, is not Tibet patently part of China, are not the Welsh and the English equally British? Not to the peoples on the ground, they aren't, and in Palestine, in Tibet and in Wales the indigenes have painfully tried to discover ways out of their dilemma. Will cultural autonomy be enough to enable a people to keep its identity, or must there be political autonomy too? Can it be achieved by peaceful politics, or must there inevitably be violence? Nowadays at least the Welsh are not fired by any religious antipathy, like Muslims and Jews confronting each other, but they were once, when the Celtic church of Wales found itself challenged by the Roman Catholic Church of England; and it is no coincidence that in the struggle to maintain their language, the Welsh patriots have borrowed ideas from the saviors of Hebrew.

Many Welsh people look rather Semitic themselves. Englishmen working in the Middle East have told me they often find dealing with Arabs very like dealing with Welshmen, but more often they have been likened to Jews. In fact some Welsh people have seriously believed themselves to be the Lost Tribe of Israel. Long familiarity with the Bible has meant that the map of Wales is spattered with Palestinian names, from Salem to Nazareth to the village of Bethlehem itself, which provides a favorite postmark for Christmas mail. Perhaps the long centuries of suppression, and the consequent sharpening of wits and wiliness, really have similarly affected Welsh and Jews, and made both peoples touchy but unextinguishable.

Certainly many an Old Man of Pencader still answers back, as Old Testament prophets might. The long resistance to the English has continued, sometimes subdued, sometimes raucous, sometimes aimed at complete national independence, sometimes concerned more with linguistics than with politics. On and on the patriots have argued, and although the struggle has never again flared into general violence, nevertheless many a Welshman has gone to prison in the course of it, bombs have exploded and scores of English-owned holiday cottages have been burnt to the ground.

If, by the start of the twenty-first century, passions seem more restrained, fewer patriotic slogans are scrawled on walls, fewer English signs are daubed over in Welsh—if on the face of it Welshness now seems less angrily assertive, that is partly because it has won some of its battles. During the second half of the twentieth century the Welsh patriotic movement made itself a genuine force in the State, and its constant pressure forced concessions out of British governments. The Welsh language, under threat for generations, was given official status and backing. New Welsh institutions were founded. Every child in the country learnt at least some Welsh at school. And in 1999 Wales achieved, for the first time in so many centuries, a modest measure of self-government, with an elected National Assembly and a *Prif Weinidog*—Chief Minister.

It was not much, God knows, not enough to stop the patriots going on and on, but it did dampen the fire, presumably what its progenitors in England intended. Welsh activists greeted it with passionate enthusiasm, but by the start of the new century they found themselves in a state of divided uncertainty, not quite sure what to do next: whether to press for more, or consolidate what had already been won; whether to defy all political correctness, and openly struggle to keep the English out, or knuckle down for a time and resume the fight another day.

They may yet lose the last battle, their beloved language may die, their traditions be forgotten. But what they have achieved is remarkable anyway. There are four principal Celtic regions of modern Europe, all enjoying different degrees of sovereignty. Ireland is entirely independent. Scotland is almost independent. Wales is slightly independent. Brittany is not independent at all. All have as their oldest attribute of nationhood an ancient language, and among them all it is the language of Wales, Cymraeg, which is the liveliest and most successfully assertive—the legacy of all those generations of patriots who have cherished, defended and developed it down the ages.

Well, you may be saying, but what about that house of yours? Be patient, I am coming to that—didn't I say we were long-winded?

The one constant, in this protracted progress of the little nation, has been the Welsh landscape. Sometimes Welsh men and women have felt that it was all they could truly call their own, together with their language. It embraces all categories of territory, pastureland, moorland, bog and river estuary, but its archetypal kind, the kind that is associated always with Wales, the kind that is celebrated in verse and painting, fairy tale and tradition, an allegory in itself of Welshness, is the mountain. It is never called a hill in Wales, and is never more than 3,600 feet high; but its summit is bare, its substance is rocky and in bad weather it can be treacherous. It stands at the heart of the Welsh patriotic self-image—so long as the mountains stand there, all is not lost. The best known of all Welsh lyrics, by the Victorian railwayman-poet John Ceiriog Hughes, celebrates the reassurance of the mountains:

Aros mae'r mynyddau mawr,
Rhuo trostynt mae y gwynt:
Clywir eto gyda'r wawr
Gân bugeiliad megis cynt...

The mighty mountains ever stand,
Tireless the winds across them blow;
The shepherds' song across the land
Sounds with the dawn as long ago...

For centuries the mountains offered the Welsh people refuge from the encroaching Power to the east, and thus became emblems of refuge in a wider kind, from all the shocks and temptations of the wicked world. Down the ages arcane tales of prophecy assured the people that their redemption would come from the hills. The Irish poet-patriots, in the days of their oppression, looked for their salvation into the skies, whence a faery-lady, a *spéirbhean* who was the incarnation of Ireland itself, would materialize to rescue them from their miseries. Welsh visionaries have always preferred a hole in the rock. Their legendary champions—Arthur, Llywelyn Olaf, Glyndŵr—are not dead at all, but only await a call to arms in caverns in the mountains.

Once, we are told, a Welsh shepherd lad walking across London Bridge was accosted by a man in Welsh, asking him where he had found his hazel staff. On the hill above his farm at home, said he. "Take me there at once," said the stranger, "and I will show you wonders." So they hastened back to Wales, and on the hillside where the hazel trees grew the stranger led him to a secret entrance in the ground. In they crept, and there in a great cave they found a prince and all his warriors, sleeping fully armed. "Does Wales need us?" cried the prince, woken by their arrival. "Has the day come?" Not yet, the stranger hushed him, the knights could sleep on; and so the two of them tiptoed away again, and out of the secret door, and into the other world of farm and mere fantasy.

Who was that prince? Perhaps only a generic hero, a wish-hero; or perhaps the poet David Jones got it right:

Does the land await the sleeping lord
Or is the wasted land
that very lord who sleeps?

All the land has its legends, but the mountains are not of equal stature throughout the country; and not altogether by chance, where they are highest and toughest, there the Welsh culture has survived most vigorously, and the language lives with most virility. The most rugged of them, and the most allegorical, are in the northwest of the country. It is as if some divine hand has lifted up the peninsula, and tilting it a little in the direction of northern Ireland, let the tallest highlands slide that way. They are clumped there tightly, jammed together, running away from England, climaxing in the peak called Yr Wyddfa, Snowdon to the English, and declining majestically toward the sea.

This is Eryri, Wales in excelsis, Cymru-issimo, where the meaning, passion and loyalty of the nation is concentrated. The last of the independent Welsh princes found their final strongholds in this severe fastness, and the English found it necessary to ring it with formidable castles—Caernarfon and Conwy, Harlech and Beaumaris, some of them among Europe's greatest and most famous castles, and all of them terrible symbols of injustice. Today Eryri is sheep-farming, tourist and climbing country, and those grim fortresses are no more than picturesque ruins, but its mountains form a harsh tough nucleus still, and seen on the skyline from a distance, or from a ship at sea, look like a rampart or a secret retreat, where old customs might be cherished, old tales told and old champions reverenced.

Several rivers run out of them. One of the shortest is the Dwyfor, which flows from the western flank of the mountains in seven tumultuous miles into the waters of Cardigan Bay, a great inlet of the Irish Sea. It is a river traditionally rich in salmon, sea trout and eels, its banks bare when it leaves the hillsides, delectably wooded lower down. Around it there is a region of pastureland called Eifionydd, good for cattle and sheep. This is a lovely smiling country, the mountains behind it, the sea in front, the river running freshly through, and it is not surprising that some time in the Middle Ages a Welsh swell, an uchelwr, acquired an estate beside the Dwyfor, built himself a dwelling and doubtless lived out his years in sweet satisfaction. The chances are that he was Collwyn ap Tangno, an almost legendary figure who emerges from the mists in about the year 1100. His house Trefan (pronounced as though it were "Trevan" in English) became one of the best known of the homesteads of Eifionydd, associated with the great families of the day, and with the poets and musicians who were their familiars—Rhys Goch Eryri, one of the greatest of the medieval Welsh lyricists, is said to have supped, played and been inspired at Trefan. We may suppose it to have been a stone-built *plas* of a classic Welsh kind, with its cluster of outbuildings, its yard and its pond and its roof of heavy slate.

The first historical records referring to the place date from 1352, and its devoted historian has traced the fluctuations of its ownership ever since. Down the centuries it frequently changed hands, from Madog ab Ieuan to Gruffudd ap Hywel, from William ab Ieuan ap Rhys ap Tudor to Robert ap John Wynn, by inheritance or by purchase, from one family to another, one generation to the next, until in the eighteenth century it came into the possession of a young Welsh Anglican clergyman, the Reverend Zaccheus Hughes, who was both vicar of the nearest village, Llanystumdwy, and also squire of the estate—what the English used to call a squarson.

Zaccheus was a modernist. Welshman that he was, he was a priest of the Established English church, and he had no time for the nonconformist chapel religion that was by then the passion of the people: When the first services were held at a nearby chapel he sent a brass band to play fortissimo outside its windows, to disrupt the heretic devotions. But he was a reformer too. He had doubtless read the works of the English agricultural progressives of the day, and he set out to rejuvenate the Trefan estate. He enlarged it by acquiring land across the river, and he also transformed it. The house itself, that unassuming Welsh manor, he disguised as a posh Georgian villa, by adding new parts much larger than the old, and for the pleasure of his ladies he made a bridle way to connect it with a stone bathhouse upstream, where they could disport themselves in happy privacy while their servants looked after the horses outside. The land he "improved," as the saying was, by drainage schemes, new walling and a series of riverine water mills. And in 1777 he erected two fine outbuildings, out of sight of the Plas. One was a coach house, for the housing of his doubtless elegant equipage, and on the roof of this he put a wooden cupola, surmounted by a weather vane with English lettering for the compass points, and his proud initials ZH. The other was a stable block, with loose-boxes for the horses downstairs, and living quarters for the stablemen above.

Zaccheus Hughes went to his fathers, and Trefan struggled on through difficult times. It was the setting for a Victorian morality drama when the poor heiress of the estate, a widowed mother, was heartlessly deprived of her inheritance. Jane Jones had married Zaccheus's son John, and had a daughter by him, but her husband died six months later and at nineteen she was left all alone with her baby as owner of the estate. Unfortunately she herself had been born out of wedlock. This was no great sin among most Welsh people in those days—we read of a Welsh country gentleman horrifying a visiting English judge, as they drove together to the county Assizes, by telling him cheerfully that both the coachman who was driving them and the footman up behind were his own illegitimate sons.

In one way or another, however, illegitimacy was a legal handicap under the English legal systems, and fifteen years after her husband's death relatives by marriage, headed by a Samuel Priestley from Yorkshire in England, disputed Jane's possession of Trefan. They argued that as she was illegitimate, her marriage to John Hughes was illegal by the laws of the day, and that she therefore had no right to the estate. After a long and acidulous lawsuit, while Jane struggled gamely on at Trefan, they won their case. The unhappy widow was dispossessed, and for the first time since the days of the Welsh princes, hard-faced grasping English folk—or so I bitterly imagine them—moved into the old Plas.

The estate became an object of contumely among the neighboring villagers, Welsh in those days to the last crone or infant, and the Priestley clan was never truly accepted—they showed not the slightest interest, remembered one local contemporary, in what was going on in the village, and "did nothing to further the interests of the villagers in any way whatsoever." As it happened Llanystumdwy was the home of the politician David Lloyd George, presently to become the most radical Prime Minister Britain had ever seen, and one of the most charismatic. He proudly proclaimed himself "a cottage man," and he was the political scourge of great landowners, so it was no surprise that when, between the two world wars, most of the ancient Welsh estates disintegrated, Trefan should go too. Tenant farmers took over most of the land, and the Plas itself passed from hand to hand until it came, one fortunate day, into mine.

"Your house at last!" No, we're not there yet. I brought up a family in Plas Trefan, but by the 1970s, when the children grew up and went away, my partner Elizabeth and I found ourselves rattling about rather in its tall old rooms. We decided to sell it but to keep for ourselves Zaccheus's 200-year-old outbuildings, behind a bank of trees to the east. We put our Rolls-Royce Silver Dawn of the day into the coach house, where it looked magnificently at home, being of an almost Georgian vintage itself; and we ourselves cleared out the horse stalls, retrieved the bookcases from the big house and moved into the stable block.

It was in a state of semi-dereliction, its yard almost impenetrable with brambles, its slate roof rickety, horseshoes and donkey-shoes lying about in the loose-stalls, and many signs of the bonfires which our children used to enjoy making there—perhaps in the hope, fortunately unfulfilled, that they could eventually make a bonfire of the whole place. Upstairs there were piles of the grain that the stablemen had used to fatten and invigorate their horses. Owls sometimes swooped among the rafters, and sundry rustlings testified to the presence of rats, mice and bats. However Elizabeth soon planned the adaptation of the old place, and a pair of young brothers from down the road, sometimes helped by their wives, did the necessary construction.

We called the building Trefan Morys, partly after the estate, partly after the Welsh spelling of my surname; and so it was—I told you to be patient!—that this modest old structure, built for livestock, became instead a Writer's House in Wales.

CHAPTER TWO

A Welsh House

At first sight, I'm sure you will agree, it is nothing much to look at. There are lots of such buildings in our part of Wales—solid old stone-built farm buildings, apparently timeless, built of big rough boulders and roofed with slate from the mountain quarries. Many of them are crumbled now, but many more still shelter cattle, and some have been converted like mine into dwelling places. Whatever their condition, they are impregnated with Welshness. Their very stoniness, their modest strength, their moss-grown stones and wooden doors—their texture, substance and style are all organic to this particular corner of Europe.

Frank Lloyd Wright, of Welsh origins himself, said of his architecture that it was not *on* the hill, but *of* the hill. His famously beautiful houses in America, sometimes with Welsh names, do sit among their rocks, deserts and prairies as though they are geological outcrops, and similarly these vernacular buildings of the Welsh countryside, even if they have been given a touch of fastidious grace by a Zaccheus Hughes, still look as though they have sprung out of the Welsh soil, without benefit of architect or laborer. My house has certainly been architect-free, which is why a buttress of hefty boulders we added to one end of it, intended to stop the whole thing falling down, turned out to have misinterpreted the nature of stress, and to stand at the wrong side of the house.

Trefan Morys is embedded in farmland, and since it stands in one of the wettest corners of Europe, its purlieus are sometimes so slobbery and congealed with mud that they suggest to me a battlefield of the First World War. If you don't mind getting your shoes messy, though, you can walk pleasantly to the house from the village of Llanystumdwy by following the Dwyfor upstream, and clambering up a wooded bank. On the other hand to get there by car you must drive up a winding, bumpy, potholed and unsurfaced lane, puddled in winter, dusty as Spain in high summer.

It is June now, so as we take the second alternative a cloud of dust billows behind us, suggesting the djinn-like clouds that pursued Lawrence of Arabia's armored cars across the deserts of Nejd. It is a moot point whether it is wiser to drive carefully up our lane, to spare your shock absorbers the worst of the bumps and the most savage of the holes, or to drive as fast as possible, so as to fly over protrusions and declivities alike without the car noticing them. I belong to the latter school partly because I enjoy a helter-skelter drive, but chiefly because I am always in a hurry to get home. It is accordingly a somewhat shattered or fragmented pleasure for me when I turn the last corner of the lane, always hoping that the exhaust pipe hasn't fallen off, and race up its most uncompromisingly bucolic slope to the house.

It's the one on the left. The one on the right is Zaccheus Hughes's old coach house, now inhabited by my son Twm, a poet in the Welsh language who runs, as a poet should, not a Rolls-Royce Silver Dawn, but a 1959 Morris Minor. On the coach house roof is its original white cupola, with ZH on its weather vane, and the letters of the English compass points. On the left, though, is Trefan Morys, and this now has a cupola too. JM are the initials on *its* weather vane, and—look, d'you see?—the points of the compass below are bilingually Welsh and English: G and D for *Gogledd* and *De*, E and W for East and West. This is partly because the Welsh names for East and West also begin with G and D, but it chiefly is a declaration, on my part, of the nature and meaning of my house.

Stop now! Do you smell it? A sweet elemental fragrance, fragile but intoxicating, that hangs upon the air? Nothing could be more fundamental to the place. It is the smell of burning wood, gathered from the woodland that lines the bank down to the river, and it has haunted Trefan always, since the bards entertained the uchelwyr in the stone-flagged halls of antiquity. And now do you hear a steady rushing noise, gently rising and falling? That is the voice of the Dwyfor, tumbling down to the sea just over the ridge there. The Swazi kings are interred in a cavern in the hills of Swaziland which stands similarly above a rushing river, and they say there that when the noise of the stream suddenly seems to fall silent, you will know you have reached the hallowed enclosure. Here I like to fancy it is the other way round, and that when that watery burble reaches your ears, it says you are entering the sanctuary of Trefan Morys. We dump the car, and pass through a pair of tall oak gates into an enclosure beyond.

Until a year or two ago, I must tell you, the gates were more interesting. They were far more ramshackle then, old boards clamped and nailed together with bits of wood, with rusted iron hinges, and splintered patches here and there. The gaps beneath them were so wide that a cat could pass through almost without wriggling, and to keep them closed they had to be propped up with stones. I loved them because they always reminded me of gates on the island of Crete, whose age-old fabrics, repeatedly patched, always seem to me to be sheltering mysterious secrets within. Trefan Morys's gates used to suggest the same, but they had not weathered the Atlantic centuries as well as their Cretan counterparts had defied the Mediterranean, and so they were replaced by gates of oak so solid that they will last a thousand years, and to the annoyance of Ibsen our Norwegian Forest cat, take a bit of squirming under.

Anyway we pass through the gates (noting as we go various anomalous knobs and handles inherited from their predecessors—I think of them as generational) and we find ourselves in a stone-walled yard. One side of it is filled by the house, built of assorted undressed granite boulders. It is long and low, with one door downstairs, and a second on the second floor, reached by a flight of stone steps dripping with toadflax. The doors are dark blue. There are half a dozen rather churchy-looking windows on this side of the house, and a clutter of gray plastic downpipes which would look anomalous to architectural purists, but strike me as engagingly functional.

At one end the second floor opens onto a deck or terrace, balustraded with slate slabs, planked with wood, and above it all rises my own white wooden cupola—well, off-white generally, between paint jobs, and cracking a bit in some places. Long ago I dreamt of settling a colony of storks in it, forever paying honor to my initials above their heads. When I learnt that their wings would have to be pinioned, to prevent them migrating in search of Hans Andersen, I imported instead some fan-tailed doves from England. These turned out to have a strong homing instinct, and promptly flew back to Gloucestershire, so in the end I made do with housing our television aerial inside the woodwork. The weather vane makes a slight grating noise, as the wind revolves it, and I like to fancy the points of the compass rustily replying—East West, groan the English ones, Gogledd De, squeak the Welsh pair slyly in reply.

There's a bold iron bell beside the door, embossed with the date 1842. We brought it with us from the big house. In Victorian times it was used to summon the fieldworkers home for their victuals, rather like the slave bells of the American South: now it is meant to be a doorbell, although since it is so stately-looking hardly anybody ever dares to ring it, preferring to knock on the door instead. We'll use it ourselves, though, to tell Elizabeth we're here—but no, wait a minute, isn't that the whine of a vacuum cleaner? She is hastily cleaning up for your arrival—there have been grandchildren about, and at this time of year Ibsen is inclined to moult his luxuriant northern fur. Elizabeth is the designer of Trefan Morys as it is today, and if for me the building is some kind of symbolical abstraction, for her it is essentially a living machine. Give her a moment, then, wait until the motor winds down, and then—Clang! Clang! Clang! sounds the big bell.

The door is a stable door still, opening in two halves, top and bottom, so that a horse could watch the passing scene through the top part. It now leads directly into the kitchen, which is also the dining room. The dining room indeed! Up at the Plas, in its great medieval days, doubtless the uchelwyr ate grandly enough, but to the stablemen who lived in this house before us I suspect the very notion of an *ystafell fwyta,* a dining room, would have seemed grandiose. I'm sure they were splendid drinkers, but anything but gourmets.

Times are changing now, but until very recently most people in this part of Wales, far among the western seas, remote from newfangled ideas of cuisine or even edibility, were never terribly interested in food. Just as the people of Sardinia declined to taste the carrot until the 1950s, so to this day many of my neighbors, living beside waters rich in shellfish, have never eaten an oyster or even a mussel. Within the memory of living people herring was the only fish they would touch. Elsewhere in Wales people subsisted largely on potatoes, and the quarrymen in the mountains ate mostly bread and butter; but for centuries a staple of the rural diet up here was a dish called *sgotyn*—break a slice of bread into a bowl, pour boiling water over it, add salt and pepper to taste and serve at once. When they were eating roast peacock and oyster pie in the great hall of Plas Trefan, their stable-serfs were deep into sgotyn, so that the advanced cuisines with which Elizabeth experiments, though thoroughly organic, always seem to me a little anomalous to the house.

Nevertheless, when we open the door the kitchen does look inalienably Welsh, because its floor is of big Welsh slate slabs, and it is dominated by a high Welsh dresser loaded with Welsh crockery. "Ho," I cry, spotting a book of contemporary Polynesian cookery beside the cooker, "What's this? Bring me sgotyn!" For my own eating preferences are basic too. I like single malt whisky with bully beef, and marmalade with sausages, but in general I hate anything too fancy, whether of cuisine or of décor—anything to do with gourmetcy or epicureanism—candlelit dinners, elaborate sauces, fashionable interethnic stuff, sun-dried mushrooms or blackened tuna. Give me sgotyn every time. I boast of having drunk a glass of wine every day since the Second World War, but young and simple wines are the ones I most enjoy, fresh from the vineyards, with none of your vaunted bouquets of leather or of pomegranate—wines, as Evelyn Waugh once wrote of Cretan vintages, "lowly esteemed by connoisseurs."

Still, the Tahiti chicken in the oven really does smell rather good, there is a bottle of Australian red on the table (no pedantry in this house about white wine with white meat), and after that hair-raising drive up the lane you look as if you might welcome more than a slice of peppered bread in boiling water, so let us sit down on a bench at the table, and have a little lunch.

Ah, hospitality! To my mind it is much better for the giver than for the receiver. I have not dined in anybody else's house for several years, far preferring to eat in restaurants, and I would stay in the scruffiest hotel in Zagazig rather than accept the offer of a room for the night from the dearest of friends ("but believe me, you know us, we'd never bother you, we'd leave you quite alone." *Oh yeah?*). Nor am I by nature gregarious, cherishing my privacy and my solitude. But I love welcoming people to Trefan Morys. Sometimes, if I hear strangers walking down the lane outside, I leap out upon them and drag them in for a glass of wine or a cup of tea. It is the duty of a house to be hospitable, and especially a Welsh house, for kindness to visitors was compulsory here long before the days of tourism. There is even a sort of folk-saint of Welsh hospitality— Ifor Hael, Ifor the Generous, who was poetically immortalized for his generosity in the fourteenth century, and is still hazily remembered in houses named Llys Ifor, Ifor's Court, or pubs called the Ifor Arms.

The kitchen has always been the theater of this style—the Welsh kitchen, where, as the poet Gerard Manley Hopkins thought in the nineteenth century,

> *That cordial air made those kind people a hood*
> *All over, as of a bevy of eggs the mothering wing*
> *Will, or mild nights the new morsels of Spring...*

It was the center of every cottage, where the hearth was, where the children slept in cots beside the fire, where the cat dozed among the sheepdogs and the saucepans hung polished from the wall. A thousand Welsh fables are set in the kitchen. Here the *tylwyth teg,* the Fair People, came knocking at the door disguised as beggars, to reward generous housewives with supernatural favors. Here strange old men crouched in the firelight, telling tales of revenge or recompense. Sinister fairy-harps appeared in the kitchen, driving people mad with their insensate music. And when in the distant past Elen, a young mother, was disobliging to the tylwyth teg, she found her lovely child gradually transmuting, day after day, into a malignant elf, leering at her from its cradle beside the ancestral hearth.

By and large, though, the kitchens of Wales have happy connotations. They were the rooms where families got to know each other, friends met and children grew up from babies to fellow-workers. When Welsh people were far away from home, it was chiefly the kitchen they remembered with fond nostalgia, and when they were old and prolix they talked incessantly of childhood evenings by the kitchen fire. Our kitchen has been a place of children too, and the house is full of their mementos: children who are now men and women, and are represented here by the books they have published, the music they have recorded, the pictures they have drawn or painted, and also children who are children still.

For those grandchildren that Elizabeth was cleaning up after often come here during their holidays. On the wall beside the door there we have penciled a register of their heights, from babyhood to adolescent: from the days when Jess or Sam could scarcely stand to be measured, to the times when Ruben or Angharad were taller than we were ourselves, and no longer worth the recording. We did it always as we said goodbye to them, and I can still remember the mingled hilarity, sadness and anticipation of the occasions: they were amused by the ritual, they were miserable to be going back to school, they were happy to think they would soon be in their own beds at home (and some of the same emotions, I fear, passed through our own minds, as in loving exhaustion we offered their mothers a last cup of tea for the road).

Wherever Welsh people have gone in the world, the image of the cup of tea has gone with them. Even now, in the days of universal junk food, Welsh women like to live up to their reputation. The Olde Welsh Tea Shoppe may have petered out but the old Welsh cup of tea, sweet and strong, is still universally on offer. When Wittgenstein the philosopher stayed in the house of a Welsh preacher the minister's wife urged her hospitality upon him with some diffidence—"Would you like a cup of tea, now, Dr. Wittgenstein? Would you like bread? Would you care for a nice piece of cake?" Sonorously from the next room came the voice of the clergyman himself: "Don't ask the gentleman! *Give!*" We have managed to honor these precepts at least to the extent that all around the kitchen hang pictures of Trefan painted or drawn by our visitors, and given to us in lieu of thank-you letters (or perhaps to mask hasty withdrawals).

Of course hospitality is only a façade of kindness, and I like to believe that kindness is built into my house. Hopkins thought the very smell of woodsmoke in a Welsh house was itself a sort of kindness, bringing sweetness to the souls of its inhabitants. I doubt if everybody who has lived in this house has had a sweet soul, and my own is frequently sour, but in principle I believe that, just as animal lovers are said to grow to look like their pets, so householders acquire some of the characteristics of their houses. The men who lived in our stable loft were charitable fellows, I am sure, good to each other, good to their animals, and if I ever feel evil tempers arising in me, I try to remember their example, passed down to me through the medium of the house we have shared.

Kindness can be a religion—what Christians call "charity," greater than faith or hope—and this was holy country once. The name of the village, Llanystumdwy, means "a holy place on a bend of the water," but there are suggestions that it refers to a river goddess of prehistory, or at least of Roman times. There are several holy wells around here too, beside which hermits of antiquity built their cells, offering cures to the sick, absolution to the repentant and, long after their deaths, bottled water to one of our neighbors who preferred the spring of St. Cybi to the taps of the Welsh Water Board. For centuries pilgrims passed this way on their journey to the sacred island of Enlli, Bardsey in English, where Merlin is supposed to be buried, and which we can almost see from our upstairs window. Enlli was so sanctified a place that in Roman Catholic times three pilgrimages there were declared the equal of a pilgrimage to Rome itself, and throughout the Middle Ages a stream of devotees passed this way to take boats to the island from along the coast. Perhaps now and then, until the Reformation put an end to it all, absentminded pilgrims with their staves and knapsacks strayed along our lane and were welcomed to beer and sgotyn by the fire.

It is certainly not long since the last of the carol singers came up from the village at Christmastime, to assemble sheepishly outside the kitchen door, sing their songs and file inside for refreshments around the table; and not much longer since children showed up at the New Year asking for pennies according to an immemorial privilege of theirs. The old customs are dying now, even here, but if we want a reminder of them we have a gramophone record in the house of old Welsh men from hereabouts singing unaccompanied *plygain* carols, ancient songs for Christmas morning. If I play it, close my eyes and hear their cracked old voices chanting polyphonically out of the past, I can imagine it is the stablemen singing upstairs, while their horses stir, chomp and paw the ground in their stalls below.

Anyway, Hopkins's cordial smell of the woodsmoke certainly permeates our kitchen, if only because the timbers of its roof have been breathing it since before the American Revolution. The substances of this house are profoundly organic. Most of the timbers that sustain it come from the Trefan woodlands, down to the river, and they are numbered still for the benefit of the haulers who dragged them up here with their teams of horses. A few, straighter and stouter than the rest, came from ships' timbers—ships wrecked, I dare say, on the seacoast a mile or two away. Wherever they came from, our beams have been matured in benign essences: sea salt, river vapor, the fragrance of damp leaves and summer suns, all marinated, so to speak, in age and hauled up here to my house to bless us all, like incense in a church. I love the woodiness of the house, which makes it feel alive, and I love the odd nails and wooden posts hammered into its beams down the generations, together with boardwood planks to strengthen sagging timbers, and odd chunks of wood to hold cracks together.

For that matter the big stone boulders of the house's walls always seem to me sentient, put together as they were with such care and skill in the days of old conviction. The men of Eifionydd are still at home with stone. They lift huge stone blocks with almost supernatural ease. They can match a stone with a gap, a gap with a stone, with an easy measuring glance. If there is one ancient craft that has survived here into modern times unimpaired, even enhanced, it is the art of dry-stone walling; old examples snake their ways over bare mountain moorlands, new ones are exhibited in mile after mile of elegant construction wherever a new highway needs a boundary wall.

Most of the Trefan Morys stones obviously came from the countryside around, which is rocky and littered with boulders, sometimes standing on end so that they look like holy megaliths. Some of them *are* holy megaliths, sacred down the aeons to the people who lived in these parts, and a bit sacred to me still. They can be eerie things—not far from here, in a churchyard wall, an ancient stone looks out across the gravestones with the chill inscription *Y garreg a lef o'r mur,* "the stone cries from the wall." More often they seem to me to possess an inner warmness, as though there is a small sacred fire glowing somewhere in them, below the lichen that often clambers up their flanks: and when, in moments of particularly ridiculous emotion, I have thrown my arms around them and placed my cheek against their rough surfaces, I fancy a gentle scent issuing from them, rather like the smell of donkeys.

I don't often, of course, embrace the stones of my house, but still the jumbled mass of them, jammed together with infinite care so long ago, this way and that, big beside small, wedging each other, balancing each other, supporting each other—the whole assembly of them, piled one above the other up to the slates of the roof, often seems to me like a company of old friends. If ever one falls off, no matter, find another one and stick it in the gap. If that bulge in the corner does seem to have grown a little more noticeable during our years in the house, getting no help from our ill-advised buttress, well, we'll outlive it, and anyway it is the destiny of Welsh buildings simply to collapse at the last into exhausted piles of stone, attended by rotting beams—a thousand such derelict Trefan Moryses litter the mountain slopes and deserted valleys of this country.

Other stones undoubtedly came from the immemorial quarries in the mountains nearby. I like to suppose they brought some of the mountain strength and mystery with them, and especially some of the wistful beauty of Cwm Pennant, the Pennant valley, whose stone workings were the nearest. This valley, down which the Dwyfor river flows, emerges from the Eryri massif four or five miles from the house. It has inspired many poets in its time. I was once talking to our local roadman, in the days when there were such folk, and happened to mention that some of our stones must have come from the Cwm Pennant quarries. At once he launched dreamily into the classic lyric of the valley, by the local poet Eifion Wyn:

> *Pam, Arglwydd, y gwneuthost Cwm Pennant*
> *mor dlws,*
> *A bywyd hen bugail mor fyr?*

> *O Lord, why has thou made Cwm Pennant*
> *so beautiful,*
> *And the life of the shepherd so short?*

So instinct are the materials of Trefan Morys with what the Arabs call *baraka*—the quality of both blessing and being blessed—that in my opinion a Rockefeller himself could not build a replica of it. Money could not buy the gifts of age, virtue and experience that imbue it, the allure of the Trefan woods, the cruel beauty of Cwm

Pennant. Nor could any tycoon move the house stone by stone to some other place on earth, as Tudor mansions have been moved, and London Bridge: My house is so absolutely of its setting, is rooted so profoundly not just in the soil, but in the very idea of Wales, that anywhere else it would lose all charisma.

Mind you—here, another cup of tea—*Don't ask, give!!!*—mind you, I fear you are sitting in a rearguard outpost of Welshness. There are, of course, countless old houses in Wales, many far more magnificent than this, many far older, but they do not represent the future of Wales, or even its present. In theory most Welsh people would instinctively covet a jumbled old house deep in the country; in practice the vast majority of our citizenry, whether indigenous or incomer, would prefer a home more contemporary. Beams that breathe the flavors of the woods and sea, stones that glow with an inner warmth and smell like donkeys, cold slate floors, echoes of lost songs—romantic fancies perhaps, but obsolete. Even in this far corner of the country, where Welsh ways are still entrenched, and romantic fancies are not scoffed at, the Executive Home is arriving, central heating is a prerequisite of civilized living, and a modern bungalow is more in demand than a venerable cottage. The remote old farmsteads, up high mountain valleys, are abandoned one by one, and all too many young people run away to the towns.

I live, though, in a Wales of my own, a Wales in the mind, grand with high memories, poignant with melancholy. It is in that Wales, that imperishable Wales, that my house prospers. When, in the 1990s, I was elected to membership of the Welsh National Gorsedd of Bards, the highest literary award within the gift of Wales, and my proudest honor, inevitably I gave myself the bardic name of Jan Trefan. Fortunately close around us many another household shares my dream citizenship. Across the lane is Twm, who lives, thinks and breathes in the Welsh language, and writes his verse in the strict alliterative meters of classical Welsh poesy, and sprinkled through the neighboring countryside are neighbors, friends and colleagues whose roots and preferences run just as deep in Welsh tradition.

Poets have always abounded here—in 1568 an earlier Morris of Eifionydd, Morus Dwyfach, was acclaimed the best in Wales—and literature is still much respected. Down the road in Llanystumdwy the house where Lloyd George died is now a residential writing school, where eminent litterateurs come to teach, and brave enthusiasts to study the art of writing in both Welsh and English. In every issue of our Welsh-language country newspaper residents of farm and village contribute their poetry, often in the epigrammatical form called the *englyn,* or in other fiendishly complicated metrical and alliterative forms of traditional bardic verse. Eisteddfods, the traditional literary and musical festivals of Wales, flourish still in many country villages; when the peripatetic National Eisteddfod, the biggest of them all, is held in our part of Wales there is hardly a Welsh soul I know who doesn't take a day or two off to attend it.

So the culture fights on. I would guess that many of our guests at Trefan Morys, who often drop in just for a cup of tea, a beer and a chat, are virtually indistinguishable from callers at Plas Trefan many generations ago. Their language is the same, their tastes are the same, their humor is the same, and I think many of them probably look the same: shortish, broad, sturdy people, the women sometimes with wide-apart eyes and sweet expressions, the men sometimes prickly with beard, wearing old knockabout hats and rugged boots. They love to talk, and they love to sing too, especially when the beer is in them. Sometimes when Twm and his merry wife, Sioned, have musician friends in across the lane, we hear them singing and laughing to the harp, drum and piano almost until the dawn breaks.

If Rhys Goch Eryri was a respected guest at the old Plas Trefan, at Trefan Morys an honored visitor was R. S. Thomas, perhaps the greatest Welsh poet writing in English since George Herbert. He died a year or two ago in his own house a few miles away. I so loved his work that one of his poems, written out for me in his own hand, hangs over there, framed upon the kitchen wall and beginning to fade. Thomas wrote in English because it was his first language, but he was a passionate champion of Cymraeg, and believed more English settlement in our part of Wales would in the end eliminate its Welshness. So much that was good about Wales, he thought, had been corroded by Anglicization, and much that was harsh and vulgar substituted. He was another Old Man of Pencader!

English people often thought Thomas arrogant and curmudgeonly, but he was anything but racist, and I suspect at heart he regretted the circumstances that made him seem intolerant and boorish. He was really a very kind man. Like Zaccheus Hughes he was a priest of the Anglican church, but I think his true god was Nature itself, particularly as manifested in the life of the birds. Perhaps it was in disillusionment that he turned back to the elementals: the woods, the hills, the skylarks, the drifting sound of an old language, what he once called, in a moment of despondency, the bones of a dead culture. He was active in the patriotic cause almost until the day he died, and in my opinion his work is the greater for the sad tension that informs it—the sense of yearning for some nobler condition that is endemic among the Cymry Cymraeg.

I last set eyes on R. S. Thomas standing all alone beside our coastal road gazing silently into an adjacent wood, as though communing with the crows and blackbirds in its branches; tourists driving by, I noticed, stared at him without much interest, or perhaps with a giggle, for he was a strange figure there. When I got home I wrote a little poem about the encounter, and it turned out to be my own irreverent epitaph to a good man and a great poet:

He stood there like an old idol,
Raised from a stony bed.
The strangers sneered, and would be no wiser,
If ever they read
What he said.
But the birds in the wood understood him,
And shat reverently
And affectionately
On his head.

Whenever I recall him at the roadside that day, looking silently into the trees as though the answer to all things was to be found among them, the memory gives me a sense of calm and liberation, as Wales itself does, when it is happy.

All these familiars of ours are very good people. They are also proud people, like my own paternal forebears. I don't think my father's pedigree can be traced very far back, but many of my neighbors' lines can. The family that now farms the Trefan lands has a recorded ancestry at least as old as Llywelyn the Last, and many others keep beneath the bed one of the majestic old Welsh genealogies, by which through long rosters of ab-Ifors, ap-Gwyns, ap-Gruffudds or ab-Owains they can watch their own seed developing down the centuries. They have been here for ever, they know just who they are, and this has given them a stately advantage in dealing with their various kinds of invader—it must be hard to patronize a Welshman so secure in his own land and history.

They are not always scrupulously stately in petty matters—they don't always turn up on time, they don't invariably finish a job (or even start it)—but they are good and proud at the heart of them. I know at least half a dozen families in Eifionydd to whom I would entrust my life: I know for absolute certain that if my family and I were ever in trouble, they would instantly be there to help us, and I hope that by setting us their high example, they have ensured that we would always be there to help them, too. Whatever I have done at Trefan Morys, however outrageously I have behaved, however notoriety has nagged at me, I have never lost a friend. Gerallt Gymro, Geraldus the Welshman, a famous Welsh-Norman chronicler of the twelfth century, wrote that there were no better men than the best of the Welsh, and no worse men than the worst. It is still true, I think, but fortunately I have little to do with the bad ones.

With such people to frequent it, and such neighbors all around, Trefan Morys remains ineluctably Welsh. It may be in rearguard, but it is by no means alone. You might not think it in the towns and tourist areas of Wales, where Anglicization is rampant and you hardly hear a word of the Welsh language from one month to another, but up many a lane like ours, in countless muddy pasturelands, houses like mine are still bucking the odds. How could it be otherwise here? Come to the door for a moment—for God's sake, Ibsen, get out of the way—here, look. Those mountains behind the trees, across the river, are called Yr Eifl, transmuted by the English long ago into The Rivals: up there some stone age people built themselves a village—come here a bit, you can see where it was—that bump on the ridge there, that's Tre'r Ceiri, the Town of Giants. And over the trees the other way is the mass of Eryri, the very heartland of Welshness. In one of those ridges Owain Glyndŵr lies sleeping with his hand on his sword; if the clouds were clear you could see the summit of Yr Wyddfa itself, the legendary Snowdon, for centuries as mystic and inaccessible to the people of these parts as Everest was to the Sherpas around its feet. And out at sea, which is only a mile or two away, are the five strange rock ridges known to legend as the Sarnau, the Causeways, relics of a lost Atlantean province which once connected Wales with Ireland—fabulous highways of the ocean where once the warrior-princes rode, with horses caparisoned in gold and women of great beauty.

The very matter of Wales is all around us, for us to see and feel and dream about. And we haven't even left the kitchen!

Actually most visitors, when they enter the kitchen of my house, think that's the whole of it. It looks much like the living room of any Welsh cottage of Victorian times, except perhaps for a few incongruous objects (an electric toaster, an outboard motor clamped to the arm of a wooden settle) and a few anomalous absences (no framed texts from the Book of Ecclesiastes or portraits of Mr. Gladstone). There is a grandfather clock, a row of gum boots on wooden pegs, a fishing rod on hooks, a clump of walking sticks, colorful plates on the dresser and a kettle steaming on the stove.

In a way it *is* the whole of the house, too, because it is the core or nucleus of its living accommodation. The door that looks like a cupboard door, over there beside the stick-stand, actually leads into Elizabeth's bedroom and shower room. The iron spiral staircase across the room, with a pebble from the nearest beach jammed below to keep it standing, leads to a landing upstairs, and thence to my bedroom and bathroom. Do you recall those apartment schemes of the 1960s, which were built of separate, self-contained and removable modules? This part of Trefan Morys is such a module. It is not separate and it is certainly not removable, but it is self-contained. I like to think of it as a sort of little hotel, into which I can fall whenever I return exhausted from some journey: hot water is ready for a bath, food is in the freezer, the cooker only needs turning on, there's a telephone on the wall for me to tell everybody I'm home, the mail is on the table, a comfortable bed awaits me upstairs and all life's intrusions can wait until tomorrow, out of sight and out of mind somewhere in the rest of the house.

Mutatis mutandis, the Welsh cottage offered the same welcoming comforts to the shepherd coming off the mountain. He may have been offered only a bowl of sgotyn, and he had to boil a caldron for his bath, but I'm sure he felt more or less as I always do, when I open that blue stable door, feel the warmth and the fragrances, look forward to the ham-and-eggs of our kitchen—oh, and find upon the table the mail left there by the postman, as he has left it for years and years. For half the pleasure of a house like mine, in a place like ours, is its sense of intimacy with the community around. Life may be getting more impersonal in most parts of the world, but still Bob the postman walks freely into our kitchen to leave my letters on the table, stopping for a chat if there is anyone around, and not turning a hair when, a year or two ago, I happened to be walking down the stairs stark naked just as he opened the stable door. In this Welsh society all are friends, or alternatively enemies—there is still little of that frigid restraint which so often marks the social relationships of the English.

I try not to believe in race, only in the effects of history and environment, but sometimes I cannot help feeling that the age-old strain of the Celts, the original Welsh, is still apparent here. Certainly Welsh people are still proud to be thought of as Celts—it differentiates them from the English—and the pageantry of the National Eisteddfod is deliberately, if imaginatively, modeled upon the supposed rituals of the Druids. Celts are always said to have been convoluted people, volatile, enthusiastic but easily discouraged, expressing themselves in art forms that were full of circles, knots and peculiar circles, and today our people are undeniably fluid and flexible too. They are careless about names, sometimes spelling them one way, sometimes another—two of my own children spell themselves Morys, the other two Morris, and I forget which way my grandchildren have gone. Time is scarcely an exact science among my neighbors. Their reportage can be unreliable. As a shrewd American once wrote, if truth elsewhere is more or less like a straight line, among the Welsh it is "more in the nature of a circle": to my way of thinking, for I have sufficient Celt in me too, only another way of saying that imagination is as real as reality.

For one of my temperament all this makes life agreeably sinuous and slippery. Occasionally indeed it can be so laid back as to be maddening. The mail may be a bit late because the postman has stopped off for a cup of tea up the lane. Iwan and his family, whom we are expecting for drinks this evening, may not bother to turn up because Megan has homework to do, or alternatively may cheerfully arrive half an hour early. Sweet Blodwen, having assured us she would be here on Thursday morning for coffee, rings on Thursday afternoon to say she was so sorry to have had to go to Pwllheli for a hairdressing appointment. How many times have we telephoned dear Mr. Edwards to come and cure the leak in Elizabeth's ceiling? What a relief it would have been if Mr. Roberts the plumber had put the taps on consistently, so that we could be quite sure that hot water was going to emerge from the left-hand tap, cold water from the right. Do you see that wooden corner cupboard? Wil the carpenter made that for us ten years ago. Although I often meet him in the street he still hasn't bothered to send the bill, but a Christmas or two ago he did send us a framed poem imagining how much happier the world would be if it were inhabited entirely by friends.

O, the charms are well worth the annoyances! Who would not rather deal with a friend than a tradesman? Wil knows for sure that when he does get around to giving me a bill, he will be paid in cash so as not to trouble the Inland Revenue, and however delayed the postman is with the morning mail, his merry eruption through the door in his bright red-and-yellow raincoat, with his inevitable caustic quip about weather forecasts or the state of the world economy, is a true shot in the arm. Cymru stands for comradeship, and in such a Welsh rural company as ours a sense of the comradely is certainly inescapable. When, thirty years ago, I did the unimaginable and went through what is vulgarly known as a change of sex, the Wils, the Mr. Owens, the

Blodwens, the mailman and the family up the lane took it all easily in their stride, and from that day to this have kindly pretended that nothing ever happened.

We live in intimacy with animals, too. As a matter of fact the ultimate Welsh animal, albeit a chimerical one, began his career not far from Trefan Morys. Today the red dragon is the national symbol of Wales, ubiquitous, unmistakable, emblazoned on our flag and exploited in a thousand guises—on bumper stickers, on advertising posters, on beer mats, on mugs, blown up as children's balloons or molded into souvenir door knockers. Rapscallions dress up as the red dragon at rugby matches. The red dragon is as essential to comic strips as he is to political cartoons.

He first emerged from the earth, though, up the road from here. The prince Gwrtheyrn decided to build himself a new capital in the mountains, but no sooner had his men started work than they found all their building materials miraculously disappearing. Time and again they tried, and time again the stones vanished. Merlin the magician was called in, and on his advice they dug a hole in the ground beneath. Lo, there beside a pool they found two dragons fighting—one white, one red. The white dragon was Saxon, the magician told them, the red dragon was Welsh, and they would always be fighting there until the red dragon was triumphant. In the meantime Gwrtheyrn must build his city somewhere else. So it is that to this day there is no house upon that spot, and so it is that in one window of Trefan Morys, facing the lane, a wooden red dragon raises a claw and sticks out a forked tongue (although according to one of the recondite Triads, medieval Welsh mantras, he should be one of the Three Things One Does Well To Hide).

Welsh lore and poetical vision is full of creature images—the symbolical crow, the celestial nightingale, the sinewy salmon, birds as love-messengers, dogs that emerge from hell, glorious horses, canny foxes, goats as military mascots, omniscient owls and inscrutable toads. They were the symptoms of a people's profound affinity with the land—a people remote from the affairs of the greater world, but close to their neighbors the birds and beasts. Most nations have their nature poets, of course, who see heaven in a wildflower, but in Wales this preoccupation with the animal kingdom has had to it a kind of poignancy, because so often it has been the reflection of national impotence. Only the wild creatures, it seems to say, are on our side in our endless struggle to be ourselves, only the swallow can be trusted to carry our messages, or the owl to advise us justly. The birds and the animals became, in their allusive way, images of patriotism, and here at Trefan Morys I am always proud to have them about.

Actually we could hardly *not* have them about. In the countrysides of Wales there is scarcely a prospect, wild or tame, that does not contain its quota of beasts, from the millions of sheep in the hillsides to the cattle in the lowland fields and the black-and-white dogs which come out barking, in greeting or in threat, at almost every farm you pass. Generally speaking animals have been favored in this country, too, at least since the last wolf was eliminated in the 1600s. Among the valleys of the south you still occasionally see aged pit-ponies, long since retired from their drear underground careers, cherished as family friends. In the old days mining families habitually kept a pig in the backyard, and genuine was the mourning when, slaughtered at the last, they were turned into chops and bacon. The dreadful foot-and-mouth epidemic of 2001 drastically reduced the number of sheep in Wales, at least temporarily, but here in Eifionydd it passed us by. Sheep and cattle still surround Trefan Morys, and the dogs from the farm (Mot and Nel) often make a brief diversion into our yard, panting and broadly smiling, as they drive cattle up the lane.

And there is always Ibsen. We have had many cats at Trefan Morys down the years, their demises always causing me temporary heartbreak. We had a string of beautiful Abyssinians, until their increasing in-breeding seemed to make them insufficiently resilient for the rural life: Theo, Menelik, Solomon, Prester John, all named after historical or legendary emperors of Ethiopian tradition. We had a couple of fine Maine coon cats, Jenks I and Jenks II, named after the original Maine coon pedigree animal, Captain Jenks of the Horse Marines. But we have never had a cat so suited to the place as Ibsen the *skögcatt* from Norway, the present incumbent. Do you know these animals? They strike me as hybrids between wild and tame, between truth and fable. They are big, tough and rather raggety, and in Norway they are traditionally supposed to be descended from the giant cats of the forest which used to pull Freya, goddess of love, in her chariot. For ages they were the prime farm cats of Norway, much prized for their hunting abilities, but in the twentieth century they became almost extinct, and were rescued from oblivion only by a few devoted enthusiasts.

By now Ibsen—ah, here he is now, boisterously shoving his way through the cat-flap in the stable door—by now Ibsen, the Nordic cat of sagas and snows, seems utterly organic to this Celtic environment. Ibsen, Ibsen, what have you brought us now? Not yet another half-eviscerated field mouse to deposit under the kitchen table! Ah well, better than a beheaded rabbit, I suppose, or a mangled mole, or half a slowworm, or the poor murdered chaffinch you brought us yesterday. The cat is only doing his immemorial duty, and the corpses he leaves for our inspection in various parts of the house are only testimony to his origins as an implacable hunter of the north.

Like almost everywhere else in the western world, the wildlife here has been decimated by modern farming. Pesticides and artificial fertilizers have done for the glowworms, the grass snakes, the hares and even the foxes, that only a few years ago abounded around Trefan Morys. Drainage more drastic than anything Zaccheus Hughes undertook has deprived the frogs and the newts of their homes. But our wild fauna is still rich, and some of it is reviving. Otters are back in the river, badgers are still in the woods, buzzards glide lordly in the sky, slowworms are in the compost heap, herons are poised above pools, doves gloomily coo, starlings and blackbirds infuriatingly imitate our telephone ringing.

The big stuffed bird that stands proudly over there in a glass case is itself a Te Deum for the recovery of a species. Twenty years ago the red kite, though common enough elsewhere in the world, was extinct in Britain but for a couple of nesting pairs in Wales. When Elizabeth came across a fairly decrepit stuffed specimen in a junk shop, she first checked to see if it had died of natural causes, and then brought it home to Trefan. We had it reverently restored, thinking it would be a sad memorial to a vanished species, but instead the red kite made an astonishing recovery, and today its great wheeling flight over the mountains is one of the grand sights of Wales. So the proud bird stands there preening its dead feathers, not as a memorial at all, but in celebration.

I respect all these creatures, dead or alive, real or fabulous, not just for their beauty, but for their immemorial allusions. I would never laugh at a toad under a paving stone because, as everyone knows, Welsh toads count your teeth while your mouth is open and you will lose them one by one. I revere the rooks roosting in the beech trees, because Brân the archetypal crow is fundamental to Welsh myth: it was the hero Brân the Blessed, bird transmuted into man, whose head was buried at the Tower of London near the beginning of time, and is today apotheosized into the Ravens of the Tower, and fed by Beefeaters. There is a local family who have claimed for some generations to have an insight into the language of the rooks, and have put some of it into writing. It seems to have some affinity with Welsh, but to the only example I possess (I have no idea what it means) there is a distinct suggestion of sorcery or even necromancy.

Ymdeflan ymdetlyn ymbetlanlont
Ymseranlont mewn beddrod eddeugant
A ddêl ac a seliwyd â seliau utgyrn ffliwitsh

Only a fool would antagonize the Toad and the Rook!

Many an uninvited creature shares the house with us.
There used to be barn owls in the stables, and very
welcome lodgers they were. They preyed upon the pesti-
lential mice which nibbled at the grain-store upstairs, and
when Zaccheus built the house he cut a special round
unglazed window, to facilitate their comings and goings.
They were still here when we came to live in the building,
and as I was sorry to have to evict them I had a little
inscription cut on a window pane in their memory—*er cof
am y tylluanod,* "in memory of the owls." A ceramic owl
over a door honors them too, and guests have sometimes
left little clay owls, rather like votive offerings, and a
couple of stuffed specimens are, so to speak, funerary
memorials. Nowadays the owls live in the trees outside,
and one of the fundamental sounds of Trefan Morys is the
hooting, often in the daytime, which I sadly interpret to
be the song of their homesickness.

The house itself is full of creature noises. Mice scrabble
above the ceilings at dead of night. Squirrels slide down the

roof. Bees have often swarmed in the walls, and their mighty communal buzz has penetrated our very thoughts. In the summer the odd bumblebee, poor old fellow, finds himself trapped in a cobweb in the corner of a window, and bellows his protest until I arrive to liberate him (murmuring, as Sterne's Uncle Toby once murmured to a bluebottle, "Why should I hurt thee? This world is surely wide enough to hold both thee and me."). May bugs deafeningly appear out of nowhere late on June evenings, burbling incompetently around the lights. Robins and swallows sometimes fly noisily in, to Ibsen's criminal excitement.

Any old stone and wooden house like ours, slightly damp, full of crannies, is bound to shelter many little creatures. Somebody estimated, in the 1950s, that a larger half-timbered house in England might shelter a couple of mice, 200 spiders, twenty wood-boring beetles, eighty fleas, twenty clothes moths, ten cockroaches and a hundred flies. We can probably match that, with rather more mice, rather fewer fleas, lots of wood lice and infinitely more bats. Bats are protected, and the little species we have, mostly pipistrelles, are generally supposed to be sweet and harmless. So they are, perhaps, if you just see them flitting delightfully about in the dusk, on your holiday visit to the countryside, or skimming so agilely over the surface of the river. If you actually share a house with them, they are less endearing.

Our bat population varies. I have known ninety pipistrelles to swoop out of their holes above the kitchen door when evening comes. I have counted forty-six whizzing and flitting around the upstairs rooms. They can be exciting to watch, but they are no fun as co-inhabitants. I have to cover my bedroom windows with wire mesh, to prevent them coming in, and after their winter hibernation they can leave an all too pungent smell of excrement behind. Often I have been tempted to exterminate them, law or no law, but as yet I have only gone so far as to make Trefan Morys temporarily a bat-free zone by banging on ceilings, slamming on floors, and playing loud hi-fi music close to bat haunts. "This world is surely wide enough to hold both thee and me," quoth Uncle Toby to his fly, but even he, the kindest soul in literature, might sometimes have thought differently about bats.

Of course the language of all these creatures is Welsh, and if ghosts talk here they certainly speak in *yr hen iaith,* rather than in the "thin language," which is how Welsh-speakers characterize the English tongue. For those who love languages Welsh is a thing of majesty, so nobly defying the worst that history can do to silence it. Is it a practical survival? Perhaps not. Is it strictly necessary, when every Welsh citizen speaks English anyway? No.

But it is something beautiful in itself, like the rarest of animals, or a priceless and irreplaceable work of art. It has sometimes been used as a code, being incomprehensible to almost everyone outside Wales, and sometimes as a secret language—English people habitually suppose that when they enter a Welsh pub and hear it spoken, it has been at that moment switched on to annoy them ("the minute we walked in they started their jabbering..."). Its great virtues, though, are not obscurant. It is a difficult language to learn, because so many of its words are not related to more familiar roots, and because it goes in for mutations, the altering of letters according to gender, or what comes before: But its grammar is mostly straightforward, and its pronunciation is entirely logical. And far from being a jabber, it is a poetical language par excellence, as lovely to listen to as it is to read—and as irresistible too, at least to romantics like me, in its intimations of defiance, rootedness and immemorial age.

Welsh still drifts and reverberates around this kitchen, the natural heart of the house. To most of our neighbors Welsh is the first language of life, and there is more to a language than mere words. Conceptions, nuances, allusions and communal memories charge different vocabularies in different ways, so that a horse, say, when summoned into the imagination in the English language, gallops away in one motion, one light, and a *ceffyl* in Welsh prances off in quite another. I can remember people here who could not speak English at all: Now everybody is bilingual, but a marvelous transformation overcomes the Parrys, the Williamses, the Owens and the Robertses when they switch from *yr iaith fain* to *yr hen iaith.*

Instantly they are vitalized, and conversations which have been lumpish or prosaic are charged with humor and quick intelligence. It is as though the ancient genius of the country, cherished by the poets and scholars of other ages, but half-stifled during the centuries of English domination, is suddenly rejuvenated and brought into the light again. Merry evenings were undoubtedly enjoyed around the tables of Trefan Morys, when the farm lads lived here long ago, and merry evenings still come easily now. My own Welsh is too simple to tap the depths of this half-hidden folk-brilliance, but when Twm comes over with his Sioned, and a handful of friends sit where you are sitting, with liquor to keep them in form, Rhys Goch Eryri himself would still feel at home.

One of the hottest of all Welsh patriots, the nineteenth century Lady Llanover of Gwent, allowed not a word of English to be spoken in her kitchen. Although her husband Benjamin was an absolute Englishman—as

Commissioner of Works in London he gave his name to Big Ben the clock—she dressed her servants in Old Welsh Costumes of her own design, employed domestic harpers and stuck over her doorway some lines which she had allegedly translated from the Old Welsh, but which I suspect she had composed herself:

Who art thou, visitor?
If friend, welcome of the heart to thee:
If stranger, hospitality shall meet thee:
If enemy, courtesy shall imprison thee.

Whoever wrote them, I like to think my kitchen subscribes to their sentiments (except perhaps the bit about the enemy—it does not invariably respond courteously to busybody officials, intrusive evangelists or abrasive ramblers, and I dare say Lady Llanover's kitchen didn't really, either). Certainly the room always offers me a welcome of the heart which I like to think reaches me out of its own generations of hospitable inhabitants, and for that matter out of Wales itself.

I agree with another earlier Morris of these parts, the seventeenth-century Iorwerth Morus, who was a cattle drover by trade, and spent much of his time away from home. This is what he wrote about returning to the kitchen at his own house, Hafod Lom:

Mi af oddi yma i'r Hafod Lom,
Er bod hi'n drom o siwrne,
Mi gaf yno ganu cainc
Ac eistedd ar fainc y simdde,
Ac ond odid dyna'r fan
Y byddaf tan y bore.

I'll go from here to Hafod Lom,
Although it's a long journey,
There I shall get to singing a song
Sitting in the chimney-seat,
And probably that's the place
I shall be until morning.

I have always led a peripatetic life, too, half the time away from home, and no moments of it have been happier than those which bring me flying up that rubble-littered lane, ignoring a sudden rattle somewhere behind the steering wheel, to scrape perilously between the gates of Trefan Morys (it didn't matter with the dear old ones, which bore the scars of a thousand misjudgments), and stand once more before that dark blue stable door. If I can hear the vacuum cleaner going I ring the big bell, to give warning. If Ibsen comes to greet me I pause to flatter him. And then—well, you know the rest!

Another cup? Or do you feel like a malt whiskey? No? Then come and see the rest of the house.

CHAPTER THREE

A Writer's House

If the kitchen complex represents the unchanging Welshness of Trefan Morys, bequeathed by history and sealed by its stones and vapors, the other part of the house represents my own contribution to its character—my patina, as it were. There is very little here that I have inherited, only a few books (Balzac, Walter Scott, W. W. Jacobs) and some pictures (mostly of Wales, by great-aunts). All the rest I have acquired myself, so that it represents my own tastes and interests, and adds a purely individual, mostly late twentieth-century layer to the palimpsest of the house.

This part of Trefan Morys, its work-module, consists of two rooms, each forty feet long, one above the other and connected by a wooden staircase. The downstairs room is entirely a library, lined with bookshelves wherever there is space. The upstairs is partly library too, but chiefly a living and writing room. Sofas, chairs and a divan are strewn about it, and a black Norwegian wood-burning stove stands in the middle, its chimney running up through the roof. A heavy wooden door, with a portentous if slightly rusted iron key, leads down that flight of stone steps to the yard outside.

Both rooms are crisscrossed with beams, and both have doors leading into the more domestic quarters of the house. The kitchen and the bedrooms of Trefan Morys, the living-module, speak of hospitality and tradition, but now we are in the workshop. Only I can really assess the true beauty of these rooms. Like red wines, they need warming. They need the caress of long affection to bring out their bouquet, and a cat to sit curled on the sofa there, woodsmoke and crackle from the stove and the self-indulgent, sensual satisfaction of knowing that here down the years, watched by that Chinese wicker goat on the table by the stairs, I have given my best to the writing of books.

Those books themselves, in all their editions and derivatives, fill a long bookcase along one wall, for me to gloat over. Nearby is a wooden armchair awarded as a prize at an Eisteddfod at Cefn-y-Waun. Visitors often ask me if I won it myself, and I am properly flattered, but it is really a backhanded sort of compliment, for as the carved letters on the chair clearly tell us, the prize was awarded in 1912.

English people often grumble that Wales is too narrow a place, too obsessed with its past and its problems. There is something to this petulant complaint. Perhaps some of my neighbors are a little inward-looking. It entertains me to observe how, entering my library, they so often ignore its several thousand books about other countries, other cultures, and make straight for the stacks about Wales! But then you probably think that my emotions about my house are just as obsessive. I do go on and on, you may well think, about the traditions of Welsh hospitality, the mystic power of the Welsh language, the fragrance of Welsh woodsmoke, Ibsen the cat, sgotyn, owls and all that. "Why, you curse those poor bats, but you're secretly rather proud of having them!"

But the identity of Wales has been so threatened down the centuries, and it still has to fight so hard for its own survival, that it often comes to assume an almost paranoic importance among its patriots. Lady Llanover perhaps rather overdid it, in her day, when she devised her own traditional folk costumes for her domestic servants, and chose a dragon and a horned goat as supporters of her coat of arms, but she succeeded in maintaining Welsh traditions, Welsh culture, in a part of Wales particularly threatened by English ways. If the Welsh activists relaxed their enthusiasm for a moment, all might still be lost, and only the idea of Wales would remain to haunt imaginations for ever after.

Besides, this part of the country was for so long isolated from the wider world that knowledge of other peoples, other histories, was generally limited. A tremendous stir was created when a black slave-boy turned up here in the eighteenth century: Half the girls fell in love with him, his fiddle music was in great demand, he became an enthusiastic chapel-goer, married a Welsh wife and left behind him seven Afro-Welsh children, their own seed now disseminated, I do not doubt, among half of us. When in 1846 the London government decided to make a survey of public education in the country, they sent teams of piously monoglot English-speaking Educational Commissioners who reported (for example) that children not so far from Trefan thought that Eve was the mother of Jesus Christ and that Moses was married to the Virgin Mary. More disgracefully still, "only one out of the three best scholars," reported the inspectors indignantly, "was able to find England on the map." Some imps and urchins may have been pulling their legs, but it was certainly true that in those days most people here were very ignorant about the world beyond their own horizons, and had probably never set eyes on a foreigner in their lives. I would guess that to those children the earnest commissioners themselves were almost like visitors from another planet, so utterly different must they have been from anybody they had met before, and correspondingly fascinating. Some years ago a cheerful pair of young homosexual men from London, one a hairdresser, one a teacher, came to live in a rented cottage in Eifionydd. Nobody had met people like them. They were probably the first openly gay couple ever to live in these parts, and they were a wow. Everybody was enthralled by them, everybody asked them in, everybody wanted their hair done by the one partner, or their opinions about the local schools confirmed by the other. It was a sadness for all, and a horrible shock, when AIDS caught up with them even here, and frightened mothers began closing their windows when they walked by, in case the germs came in...

Relatively few foreigners come to our district even now, the most common tourists being those indefatigable travelers, the Dutch, who find their way in ones and unobtrusive twos into every last valley. The most familiar aliens in recent years have been Bretons, who until a few years ago bicycled from village to village, farm to farm, selling their onions; we so welcomed visits from these well-weathered strangers, and so enjoyed drinking wine with them, that we never could resist buying strings of their onions, some of which used to hang for so long from the kitchen stairs that they became part of the room's décor, and decoratively sprouted.

There have also been, ever since the Second World War, a handsome company of Poles, now aging—soldiers and their families who declined to live in a Communist Poland when the war was over, but have lingered ever since, with pride and dignity, in a hutted camp of exile down the coast.

I am Anglo-Welsh myself—Welsh father, English mother. My first loyalty is always to Cymru, but like Giraldus before me I am proud of the best in both peoples, and I like to think that Trefan Morys, besides honoring those old Welsh criteria of the kitchen, represents too a wider empathy. That is why my weather vane lettering is in two languages, the one to represent the rootedness of the house and its symbolisms, the other to express my own dual horizons.

My two families, paternal and maternal, have in the past been very different. My father's family has been, so far as I know, living in Wales since the beginning of time, bred from peasant stock not so long ago, proud of itself and its simple style, and devoted down the generations to that seminal Welsh art, music. My mother's family on the other hand has prided itself upon its Norman origins, which brought its forebears, not so long after the Conquest, to their manor house in the Somerset Mendips—where their brass-plated tombs, with armor and swords and little dogs at their feet, look as remote from the idea of Welshness as the Conqueror himself.

Could any lines of descent be more disparate? The two families first came into contact at the time of the First World War, after several hundred years of occupying the same island of Britain, and their attitudes to that conflict perfectly reflect their two cultures. Both families suffered a terrible loss in that war, one by shellfire, one by gassing, but as their letters from the front reveal, they had made their sacrifices in very different spirits. My English uncle had gone to battle like a Rupert Brooke, and wrote proudly of it to his father—exalted by the honor of the challenge, head high, with a copy of *Tristram Shandy* in his jacket pocket when the fatal blow struck him. I found a letter from one of my paternal uncles to another, though, conscientiously advising his younger brother how best to find a cushy billet when he crossed over to France to be asphyxiated. Both were good men, I do not doubt, both were surely brave, but while one was proud to die for King, Flag and Empire, the other was chiefly concerned to see that all Morrises got safely home to Wales.

Some people would say these are racial characteristics—on the one side the Norman sense of splendor, on the other the Celtic sense of place. Wales is a great place for theories of race and nationality, because it has been for so long a place of rivalries between indigenes and incomers. Of course over the centuries the several strains mingled. The Normans often married Welsh beauties (preferably heiresses), and eventually crossbred with the Saxons to become the English, while the Welsh, for all their obduracy, so far betrayed their principles that there are probably few households in Wales today who do not have some English blood in their veins. The antipathies persist nevertheless, and they are often misrepresented as racial rivalries, when they are really cultural convictions.

As for nationality, another word that crops up whenever Welshness is discussed, it is of course purely artificial. It is ersatz. There is nothing organic to nationality. Lloyd George, the archetypal Welshman, was born in Manchester. You can play rugby for Wales if just one of your grandfathers happens to be born in this country. Nationality is decreed by a line drawn in a map, a chance confinement or a signature on a notary's paper.

I have been what is generically called a Welsh nationalist for years, but only because I believe that political power is necessary to secure the cultural integrity of a people, not least a minority people; English critics still sneer at "Welsh Nats," but in fact the chief Welsh political party makes no reference to nationality, let alone race, but is simply Plaid Cymru, the Party of Wales.

But alas the Welsh, especially the Welsh-speaking Welsh, have acquired the reputation of being prickly chauvinists, self-obsessed and introspective. It is true that, like my paternal fighting uncles, they have chiefly wanted to get safely home to Wales, and I myself have suffered always from the debilitating weakness of homesickness. Welsh people have seldom been great emigrants, even at times of national hardship. There are few big Welsh settlements abroad, such as those by which the Scots and the Irish ensure that half the world is permanently unable to evade St. Patrick's Day or the skirling of the pipes. There is such a thing as a Professional Welshman, on the Scots and Irish model, but he seldom travels farther than London, where he can often be found in pubs pretending to be Dylan Thomas. Our contemporary international stars do not unduly belabor their Welshness. Unlike their English contemporaries, even now families of the Welsh bourgeoisie seldom buy themselves cottages in France, or second homes on the awful Costa del Sol.

Like me they have been too homesick, perhaps, to be successful expatriates, and although there have been several attempts to establish Little Wales on foreign strands, only two have really succeeded. One is now the French department of Brittany, but it began centuries ago as a settlement of people from southern Wales, searching out across the Channel a landscape and coastline not unlike their own, and taking with them a language that is to this day the nearest foreign thing to Cymraeg. The other Wales *outre-mer* comprises the Welsh villages and ranches of Argentinian Patagonia, where Welsh is a living language to this day, and where a Minister from our corner of Wales regularly goes to minister to its Baptist congregations. Now that everyone here understands English, Patagonia is the one place in the world where, unless you happen to know Spanish, you may find yourself *obliged* to converse in Cymraeg.

The Welsh have, however, been great wanderers, as against settlers. If you will come with me now, up the spiral staircase with the pebble at the bottom—don't be alarmed, it's perfectly steady—and into the upstairs living room, you will see through the end window Bae Aberteifi, Cardigan Bay, which is an inlet of the Irish Sea, which is a tributary of the Atlantic Ocean, which is an unobstructed highway to the whole world. It would be odd indeed if, living with such a prospect among the sheep and cattle of their shuttered mountains, the people of these parts did not sometimes feel footloose, or tempted to drop everything and see the planet for themselves. Our peninsula stood, after all, on one of the great sea routes of the ancient world, by which the missionaries of the Christian faith crisscrossed the Irish Sea in their wood-and-leather coracles carrying the word from Ireland to Wales to the European continent— evangelists who are remembered to this day as local saints, and honored with place-names.

Welsh sailors from these parts were the first Europeans to reach America. Everyone knows that! Prince Madog ap Owain Gwynedd got there first, in the year 1170, and never came back again—he was, in the words of one of the Triads, one of the Three Who Made a Total Disappearance From the Isle of Britain. You don't believe me? Well not so far from here there is an old sea jetty with a notice upon it, declaring without possibility of disagreement that "Prince Madog Sailed From Here To Mobile, Alabama"—and at Mobile, Alabama, there is a plaque on the waterfront to confirm that he got there. What, you're laughing? Haven't you heard of the Mandan Indians of the Missouri Valley, who were undoubtedly descended from Madog's brave crew? They were light-skinned people, they fished from coracles and they spoke a language recognizably Welsh—*cwm,* a valley in Welsh, was *koom* in Mandan, *prydferth,* beautiful, was *prydfa,* and the words for old, blue and big were identical in both tongues. Who could argue with all that?

Anyway, look out there now, through the trees into the sea. Away to the right is Ynys Enlli, where we are told 20,000 saints lie buried (a sort of honorary sainthood, I think, acquired by being there at all). A little closer are the islands of St. Tudwal, inhabited only by sheep. To the left is a promontory that shelters Porthmadog, once the chief exporting port of the Welsh slate trade—the slate was brought there from the mountain quarries by a narrow-gauge railway which still operates for the tourist trade. And sailing across our line of vision, backwards and forwards, ever again there pass the Porthmadog schooners known as the Western Ocean Yachts. Do you see them? They were built in Porthmadog, owned by local syndicates of farmers, clergymen, bank managers, doctors, manned by local crews, commanded by local captains. They were among the most beautiful little ships ever to sail the western seas, none of them more than 500 tons, but of a grandeur beyond their size.

They were the ships that carried the slate, the very substance of Wales, all around the world, to all the ports of Europe, into the Indian Ocean, round Cape Horn, up to Newfoundland, coming back to London or Cardiff loaded with fruits, wines or olive oil, and so home in ballast to Porthmadog. Just for a few years they made men of these parts, once so isolated, marvelously well-traveled. In 1897 a boy named David Jenkins signed on for the first time as a deck boy and cook, and this is how his maiden voyage went: to Buenos Aires in Argentina, to Galveston in Texas, around the Horn to collect guano from Peru, to Liverpool, to Newcastle, back to the Gulf of Mexico and sunk in two minutes in a storm off Tobago. Jenkins was shipped back to Wales in another vessel, but after a fortnight at home found himself a new ship and was off to South America again. The Porthmadog schooners, like their crews, were so irrepressible and indefatigable in their brief time that in June 1899 seventeen ships from this remote haven of the Irish Sea simultaneously lay below the Rock of Gibraltar.

There they go now, swift and sturdy, their white sails billowing, their deckmen waving goodbye to relatives on the shore, or even to us if they notice us at our window—off on voyages that will take them from our little backwater into the farthest corners of the oceans. You can't see them there? They don't stir your heart as they stir mine? That is because they are only dream-ships. The last of the Western Ocean Yachts sailed out of Porthmadog almost a century ago. One alone is still afloat, as a mastless hulk in the Harbour of Port Stanley in the Falkland Islands, where she had gone in search of guano. All the rest are scrapped or at the bottom of seas—except only for those phantom fleets outside my window, which I can summon into view whenever I like. In their honor long ago I commissioned a nautical craftsman living nearby to build for me, from the original builders' plans, models of three of them: And if you look around now, and raise your eyes to the ceiling, there they are, standing on the crossbeams. All three were once familiar to watchers standing in my window, and one ended her life out there, aground on a rock a mile or two from home, after sailing all the way back from Valparaíso. The two-masted *Sara Evans,* sails spread, is on the beam nearest the window: I once met the widow of her last captain. Then there is the two-master *Edward Windus,* sails furled. And on the third beam is the grand three-master *Owen Morris,* a true miniature clipper, and she is the ship whose rotting timbers can still sometimes be seen, when the tide is especially low, among the shallows of Porthmadog Bay.

I had never seen model ships mounted high on beams, when I first raised them there, but later I discovered that in Carpaccio's "La visione dei martiri dell'Ararat," painted in 1515, there is a model galley perched above the processing martyrs in just the same way. Encouraged by this example, I later put those two wooden models of Venetian fishing boats up too, and their bright red sails, enlivened with stripes and arcane symbols, and with devices on their bulbous hulls to ward off the evil eye, provide an allegorical contrast to the severe copper-bottomed grace of the three Welsh schooners. I cherish all these vessels, silent there upon their beams, and it is a constant disappointment to me that most of my visitors, while they all admire the beams, never seem to notice the ships.

You're different, of course. You realize that they are not just models, but icons of a kind, testament to the pull of that wider world beyond the gates of Trefan Morys, beyond the coasts of Wales. Ships are all over this part of my house. Propped here and there are models of an American harbor tug, of a China junk, of a paddle steamer from Gdansk, of fishing boats from Greece, the Faeroe Islands and Chesapeake Bay, of a Hong Kong ferry, of a sailing-freighter from Dalmatia, of a gondola, a bottled one of HM Brig *Badger* that I found in Sydney, and an elegant one of a catamaran that Elizabeth has saved from her childhood in Sri Lanka, where she was born. There is also a French fishing boat immured in a plastic cube, like a bee in amber, and trapped in there beside it is a single hair of its maker's head, which fell in during the hardening process: because of this irreversible error he reduced the model's price for me, but I would happily have paid him extra for the curiosity of it.

Ships sail through many a picture here, too. There is a pierhead painting of the brig *Exchange* (Master, Robert Ashton) homeward bound from Genoa in 1812; a watercolor by A. G. Vickers (died 1837) of coastal sailing-ships rocking in the swell off the Admiralty in St. Petersburg; a picture of the Isle of Man packet *Cambria,* painted on china in 1908 and cracked amidships; a colored sketch by a Victorian army officer of a felucca struggling against a hot wind upriver beside the Pyramids; a large oil painting of herring boats lying in the shelter of Cricieth Castle. The colored oleograph of the liner *City of New York* (10,500 tons) is, I have reason to believe, one of those given to every first-class passenger on the maiden voyage of the ship, from Liverpool to New York in 1888. The Cairo river scene in the bathroom, in oils, was painted by an Egyptian artist from the deck of the houseboat we used to inhabit there: It was done for a friend of mine, David Holden, who took over the boat from us, and when he was murdered in the city in the 1970s I found he had left it in his will to me.

There is a ship of peculiar rig in one picture. It seems to be a double lateen rig, with a jib, and behind it there is a boat that looks rather like a double-ended lifeboat, with a tall mast amidships. These queer craft are seen sailing into a very peculiar harbor, with a mosque in the foreground, what looks like a Chinese pagoda, a castle on a hilltop, Russian-style spiral domes and a massive waterfront building resembling a railway terminal. I know well what I am describing for you, because I myself invented these strange vessels and this ill-assorted collection of buildings. They figure in a novel of mine about an imaginary Levantine city, and when the publishers commissioned a painting for its jacket, they gave its original to me.

Do please forgive me my conceit, but I cannot resist also drawing your attention to the meticulous image of the Italian helicopter cruiser *Vittorio Veneto* at the bottom right corner of this picture over here. I did it myself, laboriously copying it out of *Jane's Fighting Ships,* but if you will run your eye to the left you will see it is only a grace note, so to speak, for a much larger artistic project. Five feet long, in ink on seven pages of copy paper stuck together, this is a panoramic view of the city of Venice which I drew during a few idle summer days here at Trefan Morys. It is a Venice squashed flat, to make it long and thin, but a Venice drawn in such besotted detail that with a magnifying glass you can even see my little son Henry hastening back from school over the Academia bridge, in the days when we lived in the city. Isn't it fun? Isn't it wonderful? I am so proud of it that I spent months going from framer to framer, trying to get the damned thing framed, until I discovered a sufficiently indulgent house decorator.

And here is another odd one. Back in the 1980s I was doing some work for *New England Monthly,* and in the magazine I came across a nautical caprice so entertaining that I asked its artist, Bruce McCall, if I could have its original. It hangs beside my desk now. It records an apocryphal event of a century before, when the Vanderbilts and other billionaires of Newport, Rhode Island, decided to invest in enormous seaborne replicas of their own vast mansions, and took them out to sea in a competitive regatta. There in my picture those palaces sail to this day, puffing and pounding toward my writing desk, domed and pinnacled and cupola'd, with smoke streaming from their tall chimneys, pinnaces on davits beside impeccable floating lawns, imposing watergates at their prows and enormous Stars and Stripes streaming from their flagstaffs. The race was won, Mr. McCall says, "in a legendary sprint to the finish," by William K. Vanderbilt's four-chimney, forty-six-room *Dunroamin.*

All these pictures have specific meanings for me, as you see, but as a whole they are simply emblems of open spaces and far horizons. Maps equal symbolism here, too. Do you see that brightly colored filing cabinet, there in the corner? I bought that years ago specifically for its colors—blue and yellow—because I thought it would represent, in its somewhat garish vivacity, the spirit of Opportunity, as against the spirit of Content which is paramount elsewhere in the house. It is stuffed full of maps from countries all around the world. Some are up to date, some rather forlornly decline in practical value as new motorways are built, national boundaries change and place-names shift. I keep them all anyway, the new ones because I use them, the old ones as mementos. On top of the cabinet that long row of box files contains city plans, stacked alphabetically from Aden to Zanzibar, by way of Melton Mowbray, and at the end there is a box of panoramic or geodesic maps, which I particularly like: fancifully artistic aerial views of Gdansk or Manhattan, Hamburg or Stellenbosch, some touchingly amateurish, some highly professional in direct line of descent from the city-view painters of the sixteenth century.

Then there are several stacks of bookcases full of guidebooks, old and new, and fifteen atlases varying in date from the 1860s to the day before yesterday—I have no interest in maps, however beautiful, historical, entertaining, quaint or instructive, that were produced in the days of geographical ignorance. Over there on the table is a mass of miscellaneous road atlases, aerial photographic atlases and gazetteers, varying from the huge *National Atlas of Wales* (area 8,015 square miles), which I can hardly lift, to a *Handy Atlas of the World* (area 196,938,800 square miles), which is about as big as a pocket diary. Finally, just try opening a drawer of that chest of drawers in the alcove under the stairs. You can hardly budge it, can you? That is because for half a century I have been more or less indiscriminately stuffing into it every brochure, handbook or publicity pamphlet I have ever picked up during a lifetime of wandering the world.

The treasures that I find in there, when I can summon the resolution to open the drawers! There are sad ill-printed propaganda brochures from the Workers' Paradises of the lost Communist Europe, all dowdy spas and fir forests. There are American pamphlets displaying couples in double-breasted suits and dirndl skirts, with ineffable sweet children waving out of fin-tailed convertibles as they swing down to Miami Beach. Here is a civic brochure from Addis Ababa in the days of the emperors, here happy Caucasian citizens drink delicately from gleaming wineglasses in the South Africa of apartheid, and here unmistakable British colonials in floppy hats sprawl in the sunshine of Down Under. It is as though the whole world that I roamed, during the second half of the twentieth century, has been encapsulated here, and I have sometimes thought of offering the whole lot to the National Library of Wales, as a traveler's ephemera.

All of these, models and pictures, maps and atlases and guidebooks, brochures and pamphlets, attached to the walls, hoisted on the beams, stuffed in such profusion into the chests and shelves of Trefan Morys, are really expressions of liberty. They are tokens that I can, at any time I want, say au revoir to Trefan Morys, jump in the car and be in Ireland by lunchtime, France before dark. And I am reminded poignantly of the true meaning of liberty, too, by that small framed holograph on the wall, above the Cinzano bottle. This is what it says:

Glasgow G11
4.10.82

Dear Ms. Morris:
Before I go off to the Carmelites (what an opening) I'd just like to say thank you to you for all the pleasure I've had from reading your books.

Yours sincerely
K. O'R

I have fortunately never heard the call to enter a convent, and Trefan Morys is the very opposite of a monastic institution or retreat. It is a working writer's house, and quaint though it sometimes seems to outsiders, rustically innocent in its style and preferences, it is in fact linked with the far corners of the planet by all manner of electronic device. Fax? Naturally. E-mail? Of course. Five telephone outlets, on two separate lines, plus a mobile. Television and radio, it goes without saying. The world wide web is on call. You would not guess it, as the wood fire lazily burns, and the kettle simmers on the kitchen range, but in and out of this house, night and day for years and years, an incessant flow of messages has been invisibly passing.

If you could hear them they would be an endless murmur of bleeps. If you could see them they would be as laser beams across the sky, flickering like searchlights, converging from the four quarters of the weather vane, direct from Sydney or New York or Hong Kong, and plunging at last unerringly down the chimneys of Trefan Morys—the marvelous precision of it, from the other sides of the world, direct, without a waver, to this small house in a backwater of Wales! Only the other day an e-mail flashed in from New York asking me for permission to reprint in a South Korean magazine an essay about a German city that I had written for an American publication! When I was writing a book about Manhattan, long ago, I was thrilled to imagine the host of unseen rays which crisscrossed the great city to stoke up its powers and keep it informed. Thirty years later just the same energizing web enmeshes this small house too. Primitive? Simple? Why even the clock on the wall there is governed by radio beams from Frankfurt in Germany, and is the only one in the house that remembers to put itself forward an hour when summertime comes in.

I always think of music as a means of communication across the continents and the ages. Try though I may, I am unable to appreciate rock music, and I have always hated the mournful dirges of medieval devotion and festivity, but almost any other kind is grist for my mill. The stacks of CDs by the door, the clutter of tapes and the tattered pile of old records represent another highway to the world at large. Some music transports me immediately to a particular place or time—*The Mastersingers of Nuremberg,* for example, I first got to know during the final days of British Hong Kong, when the colony was handed over to the Chinese in 1997, and whenever I listen to it I am whisked back to those rain-drenched farewell ceremonials beside the harbor, with fireworks exploding, and bands bravely playing, dignitaries wreathed in false smiles and the royal yacht *Britannia* sailing into the night with the heir to the British throne. Prokofiev first impinged upon my consciousness in the 1960s, when we played him over and over again upon our houseboat on the Nile in Cairo, and so did Frank Sinatra. Mozart's 21st Piano Concerto instantly takes me back to the Dalmatian coast of Croatia, before the breakup of Yugoslavia, where I loved to play it on my BMW of the day racing exhilaratingly down the grand corniche to Montenegro. Music also seems to me one of life's great reconcilers, an instrument of universal good, which is why when I am not at home I like to leave the record player on, soaking Mozart into the very being of Trefan Morys. I want his music to be always lingering in this house, drifting down the hours and years even when it's empty—there, can't you hear a melody now, not in your ears, but somewhere at the back of your mind?

I have never gone in for souvenirs—if from every journey I made I brought back a Benares brass tray, a Russian doll, some Torcello lace or a mask from Benin— if I had brought home loot from all my travels the place would look like a junk shop! It looks a bit like one anyway, but at least its foreign souvenirs are austerely selective. There are two or three Persian and Afghan rugs on the floor. There is a small model house from Chiang Mai in Thailand. There is a deep blue and yellow vase, with leaping deer upon it, from the Armenian pottery in Jerusalem, and some old silver Ethiopian keys from Āksum. There is the wooden duck with which, in 1981, Mr. Carl Danos of Louisiana won second prize in a World Decoy Duck competition. Oh, and what's this, on a table beside the stairs? It is that wicker goat, which I bought in China long ago; it has a lid in its back, and if you remove this its enameled interior smells so deliciously of adhesive that I used to offer children a sniff, before it was pointed out to me that glue sniffing was proving alarmingly addictive in Welsh schools.

Hanging on a wall is the foreign trophy I am most fond of. In the 1980s I was writing about the State of Vermont, and in the course of the job I visited the original breeding place of the Morgan Horse. This is a breed I romantically admire partly because it seems to have Welsh connections, and partly because it looks remarkably like the Golden Horses of St. Mark which the Venetians stole from Constantinople in the thirteenth century, and mounted upon the facade of St. Mark's Basilica. When I left the Vermont horse farm my host there, sensing my altogether un-equestrian enthusiasm, did not offer me a list of show prizes, or a souvenir rosette from the Vermont State Fair, but instead gave me a small piece of lead piping. It was, he said, part of the pipe through which the very first of all pedigree Morgan horses, Justin Morgan, was watered back in the 1790s. I had it mounted in a frame, together with a contemporary poster announcing that Justin Morgan was available to mares at the farm *(Terms Six Dollars, To Insure Foal),* and there it hangs now, for my tastes a truly exotic commemoration of travel.

But this is chiefly a library, this tandem of rooms one above the other, and books too are like chords or tendons linking us with other minds, times and places— foretastes of virtual reality, or time travel. Traditionally books have been greatly prized in Wales. Today the old hunger for education has declined, and the pride of books with it; but however barren the living rooms of English-speaking Wales, their furniture grouped so pointedly around the TV, many a house of the Cymry Cymraeg still has its shelves of literature, usually based upon the outpouring of Welsh theological thought that occurred in the century before last, but often enterprising in contemporary writing too. The Welsh-language culture is still a culture of readers. A poet in the Welsh language can still, on average, expect to reach a bigger audience than a poet in English. When a serious book is published both in Welsh and in English, it often does better in Welsh.

I was taken once to the home of the archetypal Welsh bibliophile, a learned self-educated scholar, by profession a quarryman, who lived in the village of Croesor a few miles from here. He is dead now, but by no means forgotten. He was a small shy man, respectably dressed, who was born in a nearby house called Twll Wenci, Weasel's Hole, and in his youth was known to everyone as Bob Owen Twll Wenci. By the time he reached middle age, books had taken over his life. His house was jam-packed, swollen, bursting with an immense multitude of books, manuscripts and pamphlets, so overwhelming that you could hardly manoeuvre your way from one room to the next. There were said to be some 47,000 in all, and he never stopped acquiring more until the day he died. Bob Owen Croesor was much celebrated as a genealogist, often lectured and broadcast and was honored with an honorary degree from the University of Wales; but well into old age he walked every day, out of his ever proliferating library, up to his clerk's office at the slate quarry above the village, where he had been for thirty years responsible for the distribution of wages.

I have never counted the books of my own library, but I would guess there are seven or eight thousand here, packed tight in their long white bookshelves, upstairs and down. I love them all, whatever their subject, whatever their condition, whatever their size. I love walking among them, stroking their spines. I love sitting on a sofa amongst them, contemplating them. I love the feel of them between my fingers, and I love the smell of them—most of all the smell of elderly American books, treasured since my youth, printed in a now obsolete ink whose fragrance can transport me instantly back to the America of the 1950s.

My books are as carefully ranked as I can manage, fiction by authors upstairs, nonfiction by subject below, and the bookcases are intricately adapted to the rooms, sometimes for example socketed to make way for an irremovable roof beam, and stepped out from the wall, like the bookcases of the Vatican library, to allow side stacks too. I am only stymied in my methodical ordering of this library by the matter of size. Books can be maddeningly un-uniform, meaning that some volumes on a given subject, which should be side by side with their fellows, are too tall to get on the proper shelves. The book tower is where many of them end up—an unsteady pile of books, reaching almost to the ceiling, which stands at one end of the library room. Imagine the cursing, when I find that my urgently needed reference book about gray seals lies beneath forty or fifty substantial volumes at the very bottom of the tower!

A philosopher living along the road here (no, not Bertrand Russell, although he lived nearby too) once suggested that I should stack all my books vertically rather than horizontally. Most of the bookcases have taller shelves at the bottom, so that if the books were ranked from top to bottom, rather than from side to side, volumes of all sizes could be vertically adjacent. *The Encyclopedia of Sea-Mammals* would no longer be isolated and inaccessible at the foot of the tower, but could stand comfortably on a shelf with its natural partner, *British Newts, Frogs and Tadpoles!* But logic is not my forte, I cannot face the task of reorganizing the whole collection, and I rather like the book tower.

I hate the word "collection," anyway. This is not a collector's library, but a writer's working resource. I care not for first editions or rare printings. It is the text that counts, and Trefan Morys offers its owner a most satisfying range of reading and reference matter. The Internet is no substitute. Is there another private library in Wales, or a website anywhere on earth, where one could, in a few moments, discover the Hawaiian word for insult *(kūamuamu),* check the tonnage of the Austro-Hungarian battleship *Viribus Unitis* (22,000 tons), find how much it would cost to rent a carriage with two horses in Bombay in 1896 (ten rupees), confirm the date of the first performance of Benjamin Godard's opera

Jocelyn (1888) or verify a favorite quotation from Melville ("the Nantucketer, out of sight of land, furls his sails, and lays him to rest, while under his very pillow rush herds of walruses and whales")?

Most of classical English literature is upstairs in my library, with many American masterpieces too, and most of the work of the supreme Europeans is represented in translation—the Tolstoys and the Turgenevs, the Flauberts and the Balzacs and the Prousts, Cervantes, Musil, Thomas Mann. Downstairs there is heaps of history, and lots of books about places, and ship books, and animal books, and books about Wales in both our languages, and a whole stack of books about the British Empire, and books about religion, and books about art and architecture, and thirty-five dictionaries of foreign languages, from Afrikaans to Romanian by way of Fijian, Latvian and Manx. The bulkier modern reference works, encyclopedias or biographical dictionaries, have mostly been transferred to the computer, to save space, but two old friends in venerable versions still occupy far too much shelf space because I haven't the heart to discard them: the eleventh edition of the *Encyclopaedia Britannica,* 1910, and a middle-aged edition of the *Oxford English Dictionary,* with supplements—forty-seven large volumes, between the two of them, and I cannot count the times in which one or another has been brought to the dinner table in the kitchen to pursue a family fancy, or conclude an argument.

Some of my books have particular associations—I don't care about first editions, but I am fond of association copies, as booksellers call them. I am a sucker for signed volumes, relishing the fact that a book has actually been in the hands of its creator. John Ruskin did not know, when long ago he meticulously signed a copy of his *Stones of Venice,* that one day my own book on the city would impertinently stand next door to his. Harold Nicolson could not have guessed that when in 1968 he gave signed copies of his diaries to his cook "with affectionate thanks for forty-two years of service and friendship," they would improbably gravitate to this servantless corner of Wales. In 1926, the year he died, Charles Doughty signed a copy of his book of Arabian travels, in Arabic and in English, for a lady "with affectionate esteem of her ancient friend"; it is now in my library, alongside a copy of the same masterpiece that I bought in Jerusalem in 1947.

Sit down, take a look at this. This is a curiosity. In 1917, when Lloyd George from Llanystumdwy was the Prime Minister of Great Britain, armies under his control invaded Palestine out of Egypt, under the command of General Edmund Allenby. Lloyd George, brought up a chapel man, sent Allenby a copy of George Adam Smith's *Historical Atlas of the Holy Land,* believing it would be more useful as a campaign guide, he said, than any War Office battle maps. He kept another copy for himself, and in it he followed the course of the triumphant campaign that culminated in Allenby's entry into Jerusalem—the first Christian conqueror to enter the Holy City since the Crusades, and doubtless the last. I don't know what became of Allenby's copy of the atlas, but Lloyd George kept his for the rest of his life, and when some of his books turned up at a local auction scale, I bought it. Here it is, still as good as new, you see, although sadly dated by history and faltering conviction, with the Prime Minister's victorious signature discreetly on its flyleaf. (I also bought some volumes by Lloyd George's favorite novelist, P. G. Wodehouse, with his bookplate in them: It shows our little river Dwyfor fancifully winding its way, carrying the ambitious young politician with it, far away downstream toward the distant powers and splendors of his apogee.)

The association copies in my library repeatedly connect me, as a library should, with distant places and old events. In 1953 Mount Everest was climbed for the very first time, by a British expedition led by Colonel

John Hunt and including Edmund Hillary and Tenzing Norgay, the first two men to stand on the summit of the world. I was there as the expedition's reporter, and I took with me a proof copy of a book, not yet published, about all the previous attempts on the mountain. During the expedition I lent this document to every member of the team, and they all read it, one by one, in tents on the mountain or at base camp on the glacier below. When Hillary and Norgay achieved their triumph, there and then I asked everyone to sign it for me as a souvenir.

Here it is now, grubby with tea stains and thumb marks, and there are all their signatures: from Hunt's calm and gentlemanly script to the stylish hand of Norgay, who at that time could write nothing but his own name, but who was presently to prove himself one of mankind's natural-born princes. A little air of Everest returns to me, whenever I take it from its shelf.

I also like grangerized copies—books that have private photographs, diary pages or souvenirs bound into them. In 1891 Edward and Marianna Heren-Allen went for their honeymoon to Venice, taking with them August Hare's new guide to that city. I had never heard of Heren-Allen when seventy years later I bought their copy of the book (fifteen shillings in pre-metric

Brighton), but when I happened to mention my acquisition in a published magazine essay I was flooded with letters about him. He was a well-known maker of violins, the author of a classic book on the subject, besides being a practicing lawyer and an eminent amateur palmist, geologist, astrologer and meteorologist. He published his own translation of the *Rubaiyat,* and later in life he wrote science-fiction novels, of which the most exciting sounds *The Strange Papers of Doctor Blayre,* about the offspring of a prostitute and a cheetah.

His young bride was an artist's daughter, and during their honeymoon the two of them explored Venice with cultivated purpose, visiting every church and making the acquaintance of distinguished fellow visitors. When they got home they took old Hare's book to pieces, and rebound it handsomely in leather to include the snapshots they had taken with their Kodak Portable Collapsible Camera—brownish pictures of back streets, fanes and street life, affectionate pictures of each other posed beside wellheads or feeding pigeons in the piazza, portraits of people they had met. They stuck in a couple of four-leafed shamrocks, too, and I am sure they treasured the book for the rest of their lives together. All unwittingly, long after they had gone to their graves, they bequeathed it to me, and I treasure it too, having had much pleasure from reliving their honeymoon with them, besides profiting from their idyll by selling that essay about their wedding souvenir.

For writers, being habitually impecunious, have to make every use of their books they can. Rupert Hart-Davies the publisher, faced with the all-too-familiar question "Have you read all these books?" used to reply that he hadn't read them all, but he had *used* them all. I have certainly used all of mine. I have used them for plain enjoyment, of course. I have plundered them for my own work. I have used them as reference books. As you see, I have used one or two of them, notably the enormous *Death in Spanish Painting* which is propping up the table in the corner, to support wobbly furniture. (The *Gazetteer of Sikhim,* though, which appears to be sustaining the end of one of the beams, and thus saving the entire ceiling from collapse, is doing nothing of the sort, but is an illusion I devised to give my visitors an entertaining frisson; just as that oil painting by James Holland of the Rialto Bridge, which seems to be magically suspended in space, is in fact held up there by hidden hooks and wires. Such are the idle fancies of a writer between paragraphs!)

I have also used my books as a record of my own travels. I have never kept a diary, but as a substitute I long ago took to writing inside books the place and dates of their acquisition. This habit has proved invaluable as an aide-mémoire. If I need to know, for example, when I was in Ethiopia, I have only to look along the line of relevant books to find that I bought Björn von Rosen's *Game Animals of Ethiopia* in Addis Ababa in 1961. *Det Store Norges-Atlas?* Tromsø, in 1994. *The Art and Architecture of Russia?* Improbable though it seems, Darwin, Northern Territories, 1962. *The Travels of Ibn Jubair?* Juba, 1955. Let's have a look at that little yellow selection of the works of James Joyce, edited by T. S. Eliot. Yes, here we are, in my minuscule script of the time I see I bought it at Bristol in 1942, out of my meagre salary as a cub reporter for the *Western Daily Press*. And if ever the Inland Revenue demands to know why I set my expenses against tax for a trip to Holland in 1958, why on earth would I have bought a book about drainage systems in the Dutch polders if I was in Amsterdam just for pleasure?

··········

Talking of signatures, while you're here, put yours in the Trefan Morys visitors' book, would you? It's volume three, not because we have heaps of visitors, but because I like to have just a single signature on each page, so that later on, when I have the time and the energy, I can draw pictures all around it, or stick in relevant photographs, or generally grangerize it. Just your name, that's all, large as you like. You'd be amazed how hard it is to make people sign their names big and bold, so as to make a proper page of it, and it's almost as hard to prevent them adding some fulsome phrase of gratitude or commendation. *"Non, non, non, pas des pensées, M. Proust!"* is how Parisian hostesses are said hastily to have stopped Marcel, unscrewing his fountain pen before getting into the full flight of his prose, and I too sometimes have to interject, as my departing guests prepare their ballpoints for action, "No, no, no, I beg you, no testimonials!"

I am fond of graffiti of every kind, from illiterate and obscene scrawls in railway stations to the exquisite carvings of poets on Grecian monuments. I like to think of them as the signatures of time. I would love to have people cut their initials on our tables and chairs, but Elizabeth is inexplicably of another opinion, so I have to make do with the visitors' book. And our visitors, as you see, have been a curious bag. Some of them have been downright unpleasant—an imposter or two, intrusive interviewers, self-important know-alls—but I get them all to sign the book anyway. On the other hand I have insisted that nobody sign twice, however often they come, to avoid the embarrassing repetition of grateful friends and relatives (*"Again!!! You must be sick to death of us!"*) that one often sees in such contexts. The only exceptions are children, because I like to observe how their signatures mature over the years, from the incoherent scrawls of infancy to the self-consciously sophisticated signatures of adolescence. Sometimes they have drawn small pictures on the pages too, and to an elementary limner like me it can be salutary to see how swiftly people of real talent progress from endearing kiddy-stuff to exquisite draftsmanship.

The book includes some esoteric surprises. Kilroy was never here, but the author of the standard history of the British cavalry was, and so was the author of the standard work of British naval history at the turn of the twentieth century, and the first Welsh nationalist member of Parliament at Westminster, and the oldest practicing lawyer in Britain (he was a hundred years old at the time). Five Sherpas have signed one page (and I have drawn a picture of their village), a physician from the Yukon another. A sheep rancher from Queensland hugely signed, and simultaneously presented me with an opal from his vast Outback estate. A composer from Scotland wrote my name in musical notation, from the 1-25 chromatic alphabetical scale; it seems to make a curious tune, but he has generously marked it *Allegro Maestoso,* and it rises in crescendo to a final fortissimo. The brothers who first adapted Trefan Morys to my use are in the book, the men who made my weather vane, the plumber who put the taps on back to front, the VAT inspectors who come to inspect our accounts now and then, all our neighbors of course, a few visiting writers, several television crews, some total strangers who have been lured into the house by the offer of a glass of wine, lots of Americans, a few Indians, a variety of Europeans, the Welsh Islamic wife of the Omani Defense Minister, an Australian who came to offer me a job, at least two Chaired Bards of the Welsh National Eisteddfod, sundry Everest climbers, a Bishop of Hereford, an actor or two, a couple of cops (investigating anonymous letters), a designer of Welsh postage stamps (who has drawn a rough of one in the book), somebody who wrote a long message in Breton, my old colonel in the Ninth Queen's Royal Lancers, members of the North Wales Association of Assistant Librarians, cats who have contributed their paw prints to Christmas gatherings—all are remembered in my visitors' book, and eventually commemorated with more or less apposite illustrations. These books are another way of recording the effects of the years, because I save an annual page, free of signatures, to draw pictures of the places I have visited during the year: It is sad to see how, down the decades, my drawing skills have faded, my application too, until in recent years I have been reduced to sticking in scribbles from my sketchbooks, really hardly worth preserving...

The very first visitor to sign my book was Clough
Williams-Ellis the architect, a dear friend who lived a
few miles away along the coast. Clough (as everyone in
Wales called him) often liked to consult my *Dictionary of
National Biography,* then in its old sixteen-volume form,
and we made a pact one day that when he died and
entered the afterlife, if he needed to use the D.N.B.
again he would deliberately disarrange its volumes
when he was through with them. Whenever I came
home, for years after his death, I went straight to the
reference shelves to see if he had been; but perhaps they
have another copy in Paradise, for the books were never
disarranged. On one of his visits to the house Clough
stumbled on the stone staircase outside. Soon afterward he
died, and since he was in his nineties at the time, his name
on the opening page of the visitors' book always gives me
a pang, in case that last visit contributed to his demise. I
did visit him later on his deathbed, before he left for
Paradise, and he made no complaint; and perhaps I made
some amends anyway by writing his particularly
laudatory and affectionate obituary for the London *Times.*

And of course in any writer's library there is no more
telling memento mori than the shelf of one's own books.
I have completed some thirty books at Trefan, about
Wales, about the British Empire, about Manhattan and
Oxford and Spain and Venice and Canada and Sydney

and Hong Kong and Europe, books of fiction, books of essays, two autobiographical books, a couple of biographies, and now a little book about Trefan Morys itself. Whether they are good or bad, flops or successes, I have had them all expensively bound for the benefit of my great-great-grandchildren; but the ones that mean most to me are the original editions, still in the paper jackets of long ago. They make a long line now, because I have childishly kept copies of every single version of every single book, even down to a pirated and politically bowdlerized edition, in Arabic, of an account I wrote in 1956 about a journey across Arabia. How old-fashioned the early ones are beginning to look! Their very typefaces, as often as not, date both them and me, and some of the American ones are by now so old that they smell of that fragrant printer's ink of long ago. Often their papers, too, are faintly reminiscent of the Utility Paper that reflected the embattled austerity of World War II, and so each successive book, in its design as in its subject matter, stands there as an inescapable reminder of the passing of the years.

Worst of all are the intimations of mortality that I discover if ever I start to *read* one of the books of my youth: For not all the advantages of experience, neither range of knowledge nor maturity of expression, can make up for the fresh exuberance and chutzpah that all writers recognize with a pang, I feel sure, when they read their work of half a century before. Trefan Morys is a house of deep resilience, but life comes and goes through it, as through everything else. The owls have played their part, and left; the stablemen have gone; the bees that used to swarm here seem to have assembled somewhere else. On an outside wall of the house there is an inscribed stone which it amuses me to think may puzzle archaeologists of a thousand years hence. Twm and I collaborated on a book, some years ago, which imagined the condition of a Welsh town in the past, the present and the future. For its jacket the publishers had lettering carved in a sandstone slab, and then photographed, and when it was done they gave the slab to me. I had it fixed to the wall, and there it stands enigmatically now, with the words A MACHYNLLETH TRIAD and our two names upon it. It has a faintly sacerdotal look. What rite was this? those scholars of another millennium may ask. Who were these priests, and what signified this lettering from the primitive past?

Has death ever visited Trefan Morys? Mice, rats, bats and multitudinous insects have certainly died here, and perhaps now and then a horse cheated the knacker's yard by collapsing in its stall. But did ever a stableman breathe his last on a straw pallet above my library? Perhaps, long ago, and no doubt one day death will come calling here again, to leave his invisible thumbprint in my visitors' book. When years ago we were changing the purpose of the house, from a place to house animals to a place to house us, we found among the loose-boxes a slab of wood with a very distinct impression of a hoof mark on it—the imprint of some sturdy Welsh cob long gone to his honorable rest. We used it as a windowsill upstairs, and the hoof mark was for years a reminder to me of the constancy of things. Lately, though, it has inexplicably faded and disappeared, and now I think of it instead as a sign of universal transience.

CHAPTER FOUR

A Writer's House in Wales

For a sense of the transcendental is, to my mind, always present at Trefan Morys—as it is in Wales itself. This is an evasive, mercurial slab of the Earth's surface, now buoyant, now despondent, as though some mood-changing wind is constantly blowing through it. Sometimes when I look out of my window it seems to me that all must be lost, that life is fading, time itself running short, so bleak and loveless does the country seem out there, so enervated do the very sheep appear, listlessly nibbling the grass. But then the cloud passes or the sun comes out, and instantly it is a very prospect of hope outside my window—life can never be subdued!—time is ours to command!—and now that I look more closely, those sheep are not disheartened at all, but are humming with happiness as they eat!

Trefan Morys itself is not a place of moods—it is solid of structure and apparently steady of character—but it is attended by a powerful numen. Many people feel it, and its presence is older than even the Welshness of the house, older than the mountains, as old perhaps as nature itself. It would be pleasant to suppose it the result of some perfect balance to the building, a structural equivalent of the human equilibrium that philosophers used to talk about. Many of them thought that the four bodily humors, sanguine, melancholic, choleric, phleg-matic, must be combined in equal measure to fulfill man's true potential, and I suppose the same criteria might be applied to a house.

Some dissenters used to argue, though, that if all four were equally represented in a man's character it would make for a dull fellow, and that one or other should be supreme. I am inclined to agree with them, but I cannot say that any particular trait is predominant in the metabolism of Trefan Morys, which is generally cheerful, intermittently sad, bad-tempered occasionally and patient with most of my absurdities. Since it seems to me to be anything but a dullard house, I look for some other humor in it, something less visceral, less definite, and I find it in that indefinable numen of the place. But it is more than a humor really. It is a mixture of wish, idea, memory, illusion and aspiration. The old Polynesians, those most visionary of pagans, would have called it mana.

I am a pagan myself, of agnostic pantheist preferences, and if I had to choose one god to preside over this house, of all the endless divinities that men have devised for their allegiance, it would be the horned and goat-footed Pan, the Great God of the ancient world, patron of fertility and a mischievous synthesis of everything mysterious, merry and fecund in animal and human life. Anything goatish suits the mythology of Wales, and I myself have long been convinced that *gafr* the goat will one day take over the world, in alliance with left-handed humans; so I particularly honor the combination of the prankish and the formidable, the peculiar and the entertaining, that the Great God represents.

The world stood still, we are told, when Pan died in the haunted days of antiquity, branches drooped in mourning over wine-dark seas and the very oracles ceased their prophecies. But he still lives in the atmosphere of Trefan Morys, and I hear his pipes plaintive on summer evenings, jolly with the plygain singers at Christmastime.

I am speaking figuratively, of course—aren't I? But I really do sense the effect of some imperturbably independent spirit playing around my house. The mana is present even in the yard outside. The most prominent objects there are generally our two cars, parked on the moss-strewn, mud-puddled slate-and-gravel mixture which is the nearest we have got to the grace of a country-house approach. You may think that automobiles have little to do with Pan, numen or transcendence, but there I disagree with you.

I often tell solemn academics or earnest progressive artists that the only things I read are car magazines, and although I do this really just to *épater les bourgeois,* there is some truth in it. As I go on to tell them, I am intensely interested in cars, because almost every aspect of modern human existence is reflected in them—the state of design, social progress, national confidence, sexual aspiration, human psychology, economic conditions, ecological awareness, engineering ingenuity—all is there, I cry, in those two machines standing in my yard, as expressive of their particular age as any art or architecture. This fluent spiel usually floors the intelligentsia, and I am sure gets the approval of the listening Great God, who has seen a vivid selection of motors come and go from Trefan Morys. We have run the gamut of the marques and nationalities, English, German, Italian, and lately a succession of Japanese. I prefer my cars to be fast and flashy, and so does Pan.

Nor is a love of cars incongruous to the neighborhood, although the general preference is for the simpler makes, without too many electronic gizmos. A century ago most of the men of these parts were, when they not were sailors at sea, vocationally concerned with horses in one way or another, and for many of their descendants the internal combustion engine seems to have replaced the ceffyl as their speciality. In innumerable sheds behind houses men are tinkering with old cars, repainting old motorbikes, cannibalizing them, bartering them or buying them for a song. The automobile sits easily within the Welsh culture. The most prominent playwright of Eifionydd pays an annual visit to the TT motorcycle races in the Isle of Man, and when Twm's Morris Minor recently needed some attention to its bodywork, he was able to pay for the job with a poem in honor of the mechanic's wife.

So the cars of Trefan Morys are perfectly at home. Our yard is not large and not at all grand, but it is hedged by tall trees—a sycamore, some ash trees and infant oaks, hollies, hazels, horse chestnuts, a pine or two—and the garden beds around it are themselves meant to suggest the bottom of a wood. Honeysuckle, the Welsh symbol of fidelity, clambers here and there, the ivy traditionally stands for permanence, and I hope there is a rowan somewhere about, to guard us against demons. There is certainly a white quartz stone set in a wall, essential for warding off the Evil Eye. All is deliberately haphazard, in keeping with my taste for mock simplicity—the kind of innocence that masks extreme sophistication. In the spring snowdrops, primroses and daffodils sprout all over the place, among scrambled rhododendrons and azaleas. Here and there blackberry brambles show signs of aggression. Ferns proliferate not in the domesticated way the Victorians loved, but with an almost drunken abundance. Ivy and Virginia creeper threaten to smother the house. There is so much vibrant life here, of plants and insects and small animals, that if I were a poet or philosopher exiled here for my convictions, like Virgil at Constantia, I would be happy enough for the rest of my life contemplating a few square feet of Trefan yard.

It is an untidy yard. Formal gardeners would hate it, and one lady, inquiring with interest the name of a plant I was nurturing in an earthen pot, went quite pale when I told her it was an anonymous weed I happened to like. There are flowerpots on the doorstep, and peat sacks, and there is a clothes dryer and a white iron bench with Ibsen often asleep on it—Ibsen the terror of the local fauna, taking time off from his murderous prowls around the bushes in search of shrews and field mice. A couple of stone sheds in one corner were once dog kennels. In the other corner the disintegrating stone heads of a lion and a unicorn are refugees from the former offices of the *Times* in the City of London. An acquaintance of mine, passing up Blackfriars Street one day, saw the royal crest, which stood above its doors just about to be demolished by navvies with electric drills, and rescued its supporters for this gentle Welsh retirement: Now above their heads a stunted hawthorn, having seeded itself on a narrow stone shelf, stands in tribute like a flowering bonsai. Two stone plaques are affixed to the house— winged lions of St. Mark, one from Split in Dalmatia, the other from Venice itself. They are modern replicas, but in order to attract a lichenous sense of age to them, for months I regularly doused them in yogurt, and now they look quite venerable.

On the terrace is an image of a symbolic Mayan jaguar, acquired by Twm and Sioned in Mexico and poised there now in sinister sentinel. There are also two sculpted busts, and these are decidedly a jape of old Pan's. A delightfully generous reader of mine in Chicago wrote to me to say that he would like to commission a bust of me, to be made by an eminent sculptor from New Zealand. He wanted to have one for his own collection, and a second cast he would have made for mine. My collection? It would *be* my collection! The eminent sculptor from New Zealand turned out to be just as delightful as his patron, and as he worked on the terrace upon my image, which everybody thought just fine, we shared several bottles of white wine. "Well," said I as he labored away, "since everybody admires your work so much, why don't you do another portrait bust for me, and thus double my collection at a stroke?" I had in mind Admiral Lord Fisher of Kilverstone, "Jacky" Fisher, about whom I had lately written a capricious biography, and with whom I propose to have an affair in the afterlife. "Until then," I said, "why can't I have an image of him up here on my deck, close to the image of me?"

Great idea, the lovely sculptor thought, and he named his standard fee, about as much as the whole of that capricious biography had earned me. "Marvelous!" I bravely cried, taking another gulp of the Chilean Sauvignon Blanc, "we have a deal"—and so it is that up there above the yard, studiously not facing each other across the terrace, "Jacky" and I expectantly stand, listening to the pipes.

Through a narrow gate beside the lion and the unicorn, in summer almost impassable because of the honeysuckle that grows over it, and heavily infested by wild ferns—through an unnoticeable gateway we pass into a vegetable garden. It is all that we kept from the walled kitchen gardens of the Plas, a corner of Trefan that I always used to find particularly suggestive because of an insidious herbal scent that seemed to meander all around it. I found it impossible either to isolate or identify this fugitive perfume, the nearest thing I knew to it being the tantalizing sage aroma that sometimes haunts the American West, and in the end I put it down to Pan. I was not surprised when, some time after we had sold the land, I looked down there early one summer morning and saw greedily grazing among the apple trees a large and virile goat.

Nowadays Elizabeth, eccentrically dressed in a kind of linen bonnet, to keep off the flies, grows most of our green victuals here—carrots, artichokes, potatoes, raspberries, gooseberries and salads of all kinds. Sometimes we are self-supporting in these foods, sometimes not. It depends on the slugs. A half-derelict shed is her command post, cluttered with the esoteric paraphernalia of the gardener's craft, cloches, slug pellets, mouse traps, compost bags, secateurs, things of that kind. Among the growing beds low box hedges are a reminder that the place has seen grander days. Flowers abound here too, all among the workaday edibles, it being a maxim of Elizabeth's style of gardening that growing plants of all kinds happily coexist (although she can never accept my own sentimental fondness for the Japanese knotweed). Lush patches of grass grow untended, speckled with buttercups in season, and close to the house there is a solitary delicate little tree.

This was given to us long ago, and we had no idea what it was until one day, on the island of Fraueninsel in the Bavarian lake Chiemsee, we chanced to see one just like it in a cottage garden. "It is the Tree of Life," its owner said, when we asked her what it was, but it really turned out to be a weeping elm. Ours presently grew into a delectable thing, never tall but beautifully shaped, with luxuriant branches falling like a canopy all around it. You could sit on a deck chair in there, cool and dappled. One morning, however, I looked out of my window and saw it had become a Tree of Death. Overnight all its leaves had gone, its branches were withered, and it looked like a sorry skeleton of a tree.

Nobody could tell us why. A virus? Pesticides? Slugs? All we could do was wait, and hope for its recovery. All one summer we waited, all one winter, and only when another spring came did a single shy and leafy young twig appear, the sort of thing the dove brought back to Noah in the ark, to tell us that the Great God Pan had been revisiting the garden, and life was stirring in that little trunk again.

Beyond the yard the woods begin, and fall away to the river below. They are not majestic ancient woods, as it happens. Most of the old oaks here were felled during the First World War, to serve as pit props, and the growth since then has been straggly and unkempt. Moss is everywhere, old leaf mold, scattered sticks and snapped branches. Trees are often felled by the wind, and left to molder among the wood anemones, or topple into the river out of the shallow soil at the water's edge. When the daffodils are blooming everything changes, of course, and the place is luminous with yellow radiance; when the bluebells come it is as though some impossibly extravagant interior decorator has invested our money in acres of new carpeting; but at most times of the year, in the twilight especially, these unkempt glades remind me of the gnarled faery woods that used to appear as frontispieces in the storybooks of my childhood—where goblins might be, or old women living in shoes, and where little people in pointed hats danced beneath the moon.

In our part of Wales the native trees are not generally stately, anyway. The dire conifers introduced by foresters, loathed by patriots, conservationists and aesthetes alike, do possess a certain lugubrious majesty, standing there in their regimented thousands as they wait to be pulped into newsprint for the tabloids; but the wiry sessile oaks that cling to the sides of mountains, as emblematic of the country as the mountains themselves, are rough and springy, like terrier trees. Still, the fourteenth-century poet Dafydd ap Gwilym thought them noble enough to imagine their thickets as natural cathedrals, where the nightingale raised the Heavenly Host, and even our straggly Trefan woods, running along the river's edge, have inspired many poets in their time. In high summer the bats flicker through them, and if you are still and silent you may sometimes glimpse badgers plodding through the twilight; in the winter their tangled complexity, with slim toppled trunks as diagonals, and frosted pools in mossy gulleys, always suggest to me Japanese gardens in Kyoto. After heavy rain the woods are sometimes mired in deep mud: I remember a cow so helplessly up to her belly in it that she had to be hauled out by a tractor with ropes. Once, in a secret corner among the trees, a donkey of ours gave birth to a magical foal.

For they are magical woods, and their tangle adds to their spell. The Green Man, son of Pan, half vegetable, half human, peers out at us from behind their trunks just as he peers through the carved foliage of church stalls and temple columns across Europe, and after dark especially, when owls hoot and there is a faint phosphorescent glimmer from the Dwyfor, the Trefan woods are like a stage setting—the woods of Windsor in Verdi's *Falstaff,* perhaps, or a wood near Athens in *A Midsummer Night's Dream.*

Not so long ago, when the Welsh resistance to English rule was going through one of its bitterest and most dangerous phases, a young activist crept through Trefan woods on a dark night, and hid in one of Zaccheus Hughes's old pig-houses a stack of explosives, for use in blowing up dams. And one evening I was standing on the riverbank when two middle-age canoeists appeared through the dusk, navigating a way with difficulty among the rocks, small rapids and winding channels of the Dwyfor. I had never seen a canoe on the river before, and in the twilight those boat people seemed to me almost hallucinatory, strenuously and tremulously paddling there in their helmets and goggles. But if they seemed spectral to me, I dare say I seemed equally insubstantial to them: for as it happened the cat Ibsen had followed me through the woods, and so the two of us stood still and bolt upright on the river's edge, staring out across the water like a couple of woodland sprites ourselves.

These woods have bewitched many people. People really do claim to have seen fairies in them. Lloyd George loved them: When he was a boy he clambered through them to go fishing for eels; when he was one of the world's great men he brought his colleague Winston Churchill for a picnic in them; when he died he chose to be buried not in Westminster Abbey, but beneath a boulder half a mile downstream from Trefan. Remember that couple of beguiling gays, like visitors from another world, who created such excitement when they turned up here? When one of them was found to be HIV-positive, in the days before antidotes were discovered, he knew himself to be inevitably dying, and sometimes at dusk I used to come across him in the woods, silently sitting against a fallen tree at the water's edge, or listlessly throwing sticks for his dog to fetch. He reminded me then of a sadder scholar gypsy, there beneath the crippled oak, absorbing the consolation of the woods while the water with the wild fish in it rushed interminably by.

I like to think of Trefan woods as a haven for all wild and lonely creatures. In the days when I owned more of the Trefan lands I prevented badger hunters seeking out sets with their ruffianly terriers, and otter hunters from

England sweeping their harsh way upstream. So far as I know, foxes have never been hunted with dogs here, and before intensive farming drove them out little hares boxed and jumped over the fields around. Pheasants still find it a convenient refuge from neighboring shooting country. Not long ago a solitary peacock came cockily up the lane, seeking pastures new.

But Pan is horned Pan, no dogmatic conservationist, and sometimes he goes fishing. He is a poacher. After dark I smell his home-rolled cigarettes, and see the faint glow of them on the riverbank, for night fishing is the thing here. The Dwyfor has its salmon, but at night the sea trout run up in the dark, battling their heroic way among the rocks to their spawning grounds in the mountains, and when they lie getting their breath back in one of the deep dark pools down there, *psst!* that's when Pan casts his worm or his spinner. Each pool on the river has its ancient Welsh name, marked on no official map, but passed down through the generations among local people, and marvelously romantic even in translation: the Pool of the Horses, the Boiling Pool, the Pool of the Great Stone, the Pool of the Big Hanging Bank or Noddlyn the Sheltering Pool, which perhaps means a pool where the salmon and sea trout can pause for a time to recuperate. Fishing rights from one bank belong to me, but so long as a poacher is a local man I never interfere, and the Great God certainly qualifies for exemption: That is why, when I sniff that pungent tobacco, and see that twinkle of light among the shrubberies, like one of the glowworms we used to have, I whisper a goodnight and walk on.

Until his death a few years ago our local doctor was a famous fisherman. There was a bit of Pan to him, too, and as he was everyone's friend, so all rivers were open to him. He had a stretch of river himself on a nearby stream, and there he had a telephone attached to a tree, in case patients urgently needed him. He was a salmon man, a dry-fly man, so he generally fished in the daytime: But sometimes I saw him down on our waters, in his waders, snatching half an hour of sport before taking a look at Mrs. Evans's varicose veins. He had left his car with his dog in it up on the lane, and there amid a neat variety of rods, nets, fly boxes and spare waders, his medical bag nestled too. His name was Prytherch, as Welsh a name as you could find, and I like to think he sometimes haunts our woodlands still.

Because of course there are ghosts around Trefan Morys—ghosts of uchelwyr, ghosts of farmhands, ghosts of poets, of poachers, of birds and wild beasts and cattle hauled from the mire. I often see figures walking down my back lane who are not there at all, like mirages, and who gradually resolve themselves into no more than shadows.

The saddest tale of this place is the tale of that poor misused heiress whose removal opened the door, after eight centuries, to the presence of English people at Plas Trefan. Her downfall was her very Welshness, at a time when the England of Queen Victoria looked aghast at free-and-easy Welsh sexual customs. Jane's story is still remembered around here, and sometimes people see her pale wan face, weeping, at an upstairs window of the Plas. I wish I could persuade her to come down to the woods, for there she would always be welcome, and it is already inhabited by a blithe and not always very respectable gallimaufry of specters, with the goat-foot god as their majordomo.

One day I shall join them too. Elizabeth and I will end up on a little islet I possess in the river down there, beside Llyn Meirch, the Horses' Pool, close to the steep bank which has immemorially been called Gallt y Widdan, the Witch's Slope. For thirty years our gravestone, awaiting the day, has stood amidst the almost impenetrable muddle of boxes, papers, duplicate copies and long-discarded children's toys that is under the library stairs. It has a text on it that I have written myself, in Welsh and in English:

Yma mae dwy ffrind,
Jan & Elizabeth Morris
Ar derfyn un bywyd.

Here are two friends,
Jan & Elizabeth Morris,
At the end of one life.

And if our ashes blow in the wayward wind beside the river, I am sure our spirits will often wander up to Trefan Morys itself, wishing whoever lives here after us, through every generation, happiness if they honor the house and its Welshness, ignominy if they don't.

A year or two ago I wrote another text for the house itself, again in Welsh and in English. This is what it says:

Rhwng Daear y Testun a Nef y Gwrthrych
Mae Tŷ yr Awdures, yn Gwenu, fel Cysylltair.

Between Earth the Subject and Heaven the Object
Stands the House of the Writer, Smiling,
as a Conjunction.

I commissioned a local sculptor to carve it in a slate plaque and place it on the wall of the building, on the lane side where every passerby could see it. So far, however, it has not materialized. He's a busy fellow, he took a bit of a holiday, he had to finish a job of work for Mrs. Owen, the weather's been so bad, Mair hasn't been too well—all in all he hasn't quite got around to it yet. You know how it is.

Of course we do, I tell him. No hurry. We can wait. At Trefan Morys we have all the time in the world—or out of it.

Note on the Welsh Language

Welsh (Cymraeg to its speakers) is one of the Brythonic group of Celtic languages, the others being Breton and Cornish—related to, but not all that much like, Scottish and Irish Gaelic, and to the extinct Continental Celtic languages. All Celtic languages are descended from the same ancient Indo-European language that spawned most of the languages of Europe and southwestern Asia, including English, but more directly Welsh is descended from the ancient British tongue which was once spoken all over Britain. In written form it first appeared in the eighth century A.D., making it one of the oldest languages in Europe today.

Most foreigners find Welsh the very devil to learn, largely because it uses a phonetic device called mutation, under which the initial letters of words are often changed by gender, or by the last letter of the word that came before: For instance the Welsh word for "head" is "pen," but "my head" is "fy mhen." It has several letters, too, that are not in the English alphabet: "dd" which sounds like "th" in the English word "them," "th" which sounds like "th" in "thin," "ff" which is the English "f," "ll" which is rather like the English "thl," and "ch" as in Johann Sebastian. All this means that until you have mastered the alphabet, and learnt the complex rules of mutation, a dictionary can be maddeningly unhelpful.

On the other hand the pronunciation of Welsh is relatively straightforward. The Welsh "f" sounds like the English "v." The letter "w," a vowel in Welsh, is pronounced like the English "oo," sometimes as in "look," sometimes as in "loom." The vowel "y" is sometimes like the "u" in "but," but sometimes like the "i" in "slim." The vowel "u" sounds more or less like "i." They all sound a bit different anyway according to which part of the country you are in, but there is nothing so confusing as the irrational ambiguities of English.

After a precipitous decline in the number of native Welsh speakers during the first half of the twentieth century, the language has enjoyed somewhat of a revival in recent years. Today, about one-fifth of the population of Wales, 500,000 people or so, speak the mother tongue; but anyway the very existence of Welsh, still defiant after so many centuries of alien pressure, is a magic in itself, and those with ears to hear find in its very cadences, speaking to us directly from the remotest Celtic past, a beauty akin to the music of the spheres.

ABOUT THE AUTHOR

Journalist, historian, and travel writer, Jan
Morris is the renowned author of more than
forty books. Her work ranges from such classics
as *Pax Britannica, The World of Venice, Hong Kong,*
and *The Matter of Wales* to the masterly essays
published in *Journeys, Destinations,* and *Among
the Cities.* She has also written a novel, *Last
Letters from Hav.* An Honorary Litt.D. of the
Universities of Wales and Glamorgan, a Fellow
of the Royal Society of Literature, and a
Commander of the Order of the British Empire
(CBE), she lives in Wales.

This book is set in Garamond 3, designed by
Morris Fuller Benton and Thomas Maitland
Cleland in the 1930s, and Monotype Grotesque,
both released digitally by Adobe.

Printed by R. R. Donnelley and Sons on
Appleton Utopia 55-pound tradebook light
natural antique paper.

Dust jacket printed by Miken Companies.
Color separation by Quad Graphics.

Three-piece case of Ecological Fiber nutmeg side
panels with Sierra black book cloth as the spine
fabric. Stamped in Lustrofoil metallic silver.